THE OLYMPIANS

THE OLYMPIANS

A Quest for Gold
Triumphs, Heroes & Legends

Sebastian Coe

with Nicholas Mason

PAVILION
MICHAEL JOSEPH

First published in Great Britain in 1984
by Pavilion Books Limited
196 Shaftesbury Avenue,
London WC2H 8JL
in association with Michael Joseph Limited
44 Bedford Square, London WC1B 3DU

Designed by Lawrence Edwards

Printed and bound in Great Britain by
Butler & Tanner Ltd, Frome and London

**British Library Cataloguing in
Publication Data**
Coe, Sebastian
  The Olympians.
  1. Olympic games—History
  I. Title   II. Mason, Nicholas
  796.4'8'0922   GV721.5

ISBN 0-907516-44-0

MOSCOW 1980

JACK LOVELOCK

PAAVO NURMI

JESSE OWENS

FANNY BLANKERS-KOEN

EMIL ZATOPEK

HERB ELLIOT

AL OERTER

ABEBE BIKILA

DALEY THOMPSON

RON CLARKE

and the Olympic reality   8

and the amateur ideal   22

and a national obsession   34

and the explosive breed   52

and the women's revolution   66

and the limits of endurance   80

and a brave new world   92

and the conquest of nerve   108

and the opening of a continent   120

and the power of ten   134

and the 'nearly men'   152

The Eternal Flame   164
Index   166

For Sir Denis Follows (1908–1983)
Chairman of the British Olympic Association
to whom every British athlete who competed
in the 1980 Olympic Games owes an incalculable
debt of gratitude.

Acknowledgements

The authors are grateful to all friends and colleagues who have been so generous with help, information and advice in the preparation of *The Olympians*. We owe particular thanks to Vincent Page for his photographic research, to Colin Webb and Linda Martin for their patience and expertise in editing the book, to Norman Harris and Cliff Temple of *The Sunday Times* for their help in providing background information for the text, and to Anthony Mason for his assistance in compiling the index.

Photographs

The publisher has endeavoured to acknowledge all copyright holders of pictures reproduced in this book. However, in view of the complexity of securing copyright information, should any photographs not be correctly attributed, then the publisher undertakes to make any appropriate changes in future editions of this book. Colour: Allsport; Colorsport; Gerry Cranham; Popperfoto; Agence S.A.M; S & G Press Agency; Mark Shearman; Sporting Pictures (UK) Ltd; Syndication International Ltd;

Allsport: 19, 26, 27 (bottom), 31, 37 (right), 41 (bottom), 42/43, 75 (bottom), 77 (top), 95, 112, 116, 148, 157 (left); Associated Press: 91, 164; BBC Hulton Picture Library: 29 (top); 40, 57, 61 (top), 68; Camera Press: 34, 75 (top left), 90, 126; Colorsport: 46, 48, 49, 77 (bottom), 106, 119, 128, 131 (left), 143, 144 (left), 145, 147, 149; Gerry Cranham: 50, 104 (left), 140 141;

Raymond Depardon: 11 (top); Norman Harris: 30, 36, 65, 69, 75 (top right), 84 (top), 87, 94, 96, 115, 137 (top), 138, 157 (top right & bottom), 160 (top); Keystone Press: 70, 83, 88, 113, 123; Ed Lacey: 10, 62 (right), 63, 101, 102/103, 114, 124, 125, 131 (right); New Zealand Press Association: 101 (inset); Popperfoto: 24, 29, 56, 58 (right), 59 (bottom); 78, 86, 89, 91 (inset), 98/99, 117, 123 (inset), 139, 142 (inset), 150, 159; Agence S.A.M: 27 (top), 41 (top), 45, 120/121, 130, 137 (bottom), 154, 158; S & G: 32/33, 71 (right), 82; Mark Shearman: 13 (top), 16, 17 (top), 18, 64, 79, 100, 104/105, 107, 118, 127 (top), 132, 133, 142, 151, 152/153; The Sunday Times: 15, 17 (bottom), 20, 21, 28; Suomen Urheilumusen: 37 (left), 44 (right), Sven Simon: 51, 72, 76 (top), 126 (inset), 144 (right), 146; Syndication International Ltd: 25, 47, 71 (left), 129; Bob Thomas: 12/13, 14; Ullstein Bilderdienst: 38, 39, 44 (left), 55, 58 (left), 59 (top), 62 (left), 74, 76 (bottom), 108/109, 111; Roger Voillet: 35, 136, 155.

IT WAS AN ODD FEELING, arriving at the Olympic Village in Moscow – a strange mixture of excitement and relief. Every one of us had been training the whole year with just one end in mind, to get to Moscow and to compete for a medal. The sports pages had talked about nothing else for months, and their predictions had all been made. But now the theories and the second-hand opinions meant nothing – in the next couple of weeks all the answers were going to be known, and another chapter of Olympic history would be closed.

I have always had a great reluctance to think a long way ahead in athletics – perhaps it's a question of not wanting to tempt fate. But I suppose there was always the knowledge in the back of my mind, ever since I started running seriously, that the logical target of any athlete was the Olympic Games. My father Peter was much more positive about it: I remember one day when I was thirteen or fourteen we were talking after a training session about the pressure of competition, and he said to me: 'Don't get all wound up about getting to the Olympics – you'll be there. You'll be going in 1980.' And he was serious about it, I know.

My personal memories of the Games go back perhaps twenty years – I can just about remember that television signature tune from the Tokyo Games in 1964, but that's all. I can remember only a few strong images from Mexico in 1968 – David Hemery's hurdles victory, certainly, and the black power demonstrations; but soon after the Games we moved north to Sheffield, and I began to get some idea of the prestige attached to the Olympics. The Sherwoods lived in Sheffield; Sheila had won her silver medal in the long jump at Mexico and John his bronze behind Hemery in the hurdles, and it impressed me even then how well known they had become in the city. Clearly an Olympian was something out of the ordinary.

By 1972 I was competing myself. I remember travelling to an early-season cross-country meeting in Cheshire with a lot of other boys and watching the 10,000 metres final from Munich in the

Olympic memories: David Hemery's unforgettable hurdles victory in Mexico City; Alberto Juantorena's awesome presence in Montreal; the black power demonstrations of 1968 (this one by Lee Evans, left, and the USA gold medal 4 × 400 metre relay squad).

reception area. For a young cross-country runner it was fascinating. No-one had really heard of Viren, but I remember being particularly struck by Emiel Puttemans and his beautifully smooth, relaxed, light style. But when Viren took command of the race he looked superb; and he was superb again four years later in Montreal, particularly in his unforgettable 5000 metres.

Two things about Montreal, though, stood out even more than that, and began to impress on me what the Olympics signified. The first was awe at Juantorena. Here was I, a thin, eight-and-a-half-stone nineteen-year-old who hadn't yet run under one minute fifty seconds but who was supposed to be a prospect at 800 metres. And there was this huge Cuban, over six feet tall with a nine-foot stride and the build of a rugby player who was looking to run close to 44 seconds for the 400 metres and 1 min 43 sec for the 800 metres. And I realised that in four years I was going to have to develop enough to take on athletes of his power and ability. A lot of the pundits were saying that the finely built 800 metre runner would have no place in the new era; it was only our event coach Harry Wilson who refused to give in to the idea that the 800 metres was about to become the province of the jumped-up 400 metre powerhouse. He said that Juantorena was a one-off phenomenon, and he turned out to be right. But what an amazing runner the Cuban was!

The other impression came soon after the Games, when I was thrown into a race at Gateshead against John Walker, who had been Olympic 1500 metre champion for about five weeks. I could not get over the aura that seemed to surround him – in the hotel, in the changing room, among the crowds of journalists and cameramen that were constantly around him. There could be no doubting his stature or, by inference, the importance of his achievement.

And in Moscow I was expected to join the ranks of men like this. As 1980 began

I had a good idea of the running preparation that I was going to have to undertake, and that it would all have a very specific date in July as its peak, but apart from that it would not differ greatly from any other season's programme. What I had not been fully prepared for was the relentless build-up of pressure that would become more and more oppressive right up to the day of the 800 metres final in Moscow.

It came on two fronts, the athletic and the diplomatic. The athletic I had brought on myself, largely because I had such a successful season in 1979; at the end of that year I held the world records for the 800 metres, the 1500 metres and the mile simultaneously. As far as the public was concerned I was expected to get at least one gold medal; as far as the bookies were concerned I was at a very short price to take them both. The pressure of being close-season favourite was already making itself felt.

This particular pressure changed its nature to some extent in the months before the Games. Steve Ovett beat my mile record in Oslo in July, and a couple of weeks later, just before the Games, he equalled my 1500 metres time. These performances tended to shift the em-

phasis from the 'Coe's a Certainty' expectations to the 'Coe v Ovett Shoot-Out at Dawn' predictions. Everyone in Britain now appeared to know for certain that Steve and I had only to step out on to the track for Britain to get a gold medal, but now the country was split down the middle over which one of us they wanted to win it. On reflection, I suppose this sort of dilemma must have been posed time after time by the Finnish long-distance runners of the 1920s or the American sprinters at almost any time, but it was a luxury we weren't used to in Britain, and it seemed to make things even more difficult.

In 1980, though, the running pressures had taken something of a back seat. Even before Christmas I had the feeling that the Russians' invasion of Afghanistan might create problems for the Games, particularly after President Carter's early reaction. I knew we were entering an election year in the United States and in West Germany, and once the threats and counter-threats had begun it didn't take Carter long to back himself into a corner; once that had happened the boycott was inevitable, though the question over whether Britain joined it or not took months to

Images of Moscow: the sprinting of Allan Wells and (*left*) the drama of his narrow defeat in the 200 metres by the brilliant Pietro Mennea.

answer, and kept us all in a state of uncertainty.

Initially I took the easy way out. I needed to get away from the English winter to somewhere warmer for a consistent build-up to the season, and I took that opportunity to withdraw from the debate for a few weeks and work out my own attitude. I wasn't certain at that stage where I stood; I was angry at the Soviet invasion, and I knew that politics and sport could not be kept apart, however pleasant it would be if they could be. But I also thought that the Games boycott was a dreadfully weak gesture, and was in effect using the athletes as pawns in the politicians' game. It felt to me like hypocrisy, and in the end I was fairly sure that I would be right to sup-

port the International Olympic Committee and try to make a go of the Games.

The trouble was that the athletes were the people whom the papers and television wanted to hear from. I know a lot of the younger athletes were sitting on the fence waiting for a lead from the better-known members of the team like Steve or me, or perhaps Brendan Foster or Daley Thompson. But I knew that anything I said, or anyone else said, could be used as ammunition by either side in the debate, and probably would be. For most of that spring, fence-sitting seemed the only sensible course.

Eventually the Commons predictably voted to recommend that we should not go, the British Olympic Committee voted that all sportsmen were free to go if their national federations agreed to it, and the Athletics Federation voted yes. I wasn't surprised at the decision, and I'm sure none of us had interrupted our build-up, but it was yet another of 1980's strange sensations to have been one minute dined and feted and lionised as an Olympic prospect, and the next described in print as 'Moscow's latest weapon' and looked on in some quarters as a traitor to the cause.

I am convinced that the great majority of the public wanted us to go, but I know some athletes did have a bad time once the decision had been made. A few felt cruelly threatened by the campaign to make them change their minds, and I do not feel that the pro-boycott pressure groups did their case much good by, for example, sending Linsey Macdonald photographs of mutilated Afghan children. In historical terms the boycott must be counted a failure, but in some ways it did have its positive effect. The Olympic movement is now more aware of the need for unity, and it is certainly more determined to resist any similar outside political pressure in the future.

Celebrations and expectations: Allan Wells exultant after his 100 metres victory; pre-race interviews in the Olympic Village.

That was all behind us as we took our coach from Moscow airport to the village, and stood for the first time among the hundreds of athletes who had suffered their own pressures and their own uncertainties over the previous months. They were doubtless as eager as we were to forget all the talking and to get on with what we had come for. I knew that what I wanted more than anything else was finally to put an end to the pressures of that year and get that 800 metres gold medal under my pillow. I was getting anxious about it, I know. I slept badly in the nights leading up to the final, and I couldn't sleep that afternoon, either, though I usually can on the day of a big

race. But I still thought I was going to win it.

I can still hardly believe that I didn't. I still can't watch the 800 metres final on video, even after all this time, without kicking myself. I clearly lost concentration, and I was in an impossible position half-way through the second lap. By the time I had pulled myself together I had no chance: I ran the last hundred or so metres fast, very fast, but it was too much to make up and I had no excuses. At the finish I just felt numb; it's a feeling that hundreds of Olympic athletes must have felt ever since 1896, but that didn't make it any easier to bear, nor was the silver medal any consolation. I felt

empty, and I had just wasted eleven years' work.

I still couldn't believe it when I woke up the next morning. Down the corridor there seemed to be more celebrations going on for Allan Wells's gold medal. The 100 metres final had been a couple of days earlier, the afternoon of the 800 metres semi-final, and I hadn't been there to see it, but I'd certainly heard all about it since. The American boycott meant that Allan was the one British runner who didn't get his full share of the credit, and it must have been doubly satisfying for him to prove his superiority over the Americans at the Golden Sprints in Berlin later in the year. It was

The 800 metres disaster: untroubled after one lap (*above left*); **desperate after two** (*above*); **still disbelieving at the medal ceremony.**

a tremendous victory for him in Moscow, though, and he fully deserved his party – even though I was in no mood to join in.

Mercifully there wasn't much time for rueful reflection. The Olympic Games weren't going to come to a standstill just because I had failed to win my gold medal, and I had three clear days to get myself back on an even keel and rebuild some sort of confidence before the 1500

metres heats. I got on with my normal training, and I managed to see some of the athletics in the stadium. I remember seeing Lasse Viren's last serious bid at an Olympic track event as he tried to forestall the advancing years in the 10,000 metres. He ran a brave race, but couldn't match Yifter, who somehow managed to forestall his own advancing years and kill everyone off in the last lap.

I saw the great pole vault final, too,

Redemption in the 1500 metres. *Left:* **the run for home. Straub (out of the picture by my left shoulder) still has a marginal lead; Steve Ovett and Busse give chase.** *Below:* **thirty metres to go – the gold is almost won.**

with Kozakiewicz taking on and beating the Russians in their own stadium, and I remember most of all the finest sprint final I have ever seen – the 200 metres, with Allan Wells blazing away on a superb bend and then Mennea hauling him back so brilliantly. in the last 50 metres. I was sitting behind Mennea's coach, and I have never seen a man so beside himself with excitement – he went absolutely crazy.

I was beginning to relax. There had clearly been some doubts in my own mind after the 800 metres, but when I got back to proper training and then into the heats and semi-finals of the 1500 metres, I began to feel far more confident. I got into a bit of trouble, boxed in

by other runners, on the last bend in my semi-final, and I got out of it, round them and away in five or six strides – my kick seemed to be as strong as ever.

In fact when we came to the final I must have posed something of a problem to the other runners, mainly because they didn't know how I was going to tackle it. They knew how Steve was going to approach the race – he would stay in touch with whoever was leading and make his move somewhere in the last 180 metres. But they must have had a suspicion that I might race off in front so as to keep out of trouble, particularly after my non-existent tactics in the 800 metres. After all, I was faster than them on paper, so it would be reasonable to

expect me to challenge them right from the start.

It must have added to their nervousness in the early part of the race when I did absolutely nothing. It was a slow, niggling, jumpy sort of race for two laps, then Jurgen Straub dug in his heels, put his head down, and accelerated, and he took us all with him. It was a brave bid of Jurgen's, probably the best race he has ever run, and he consistently built up the pace, running faster and faster all the way into the final straight. It sapped the strength from everyone – we could all feel it, I'm sure, getting harder and harder as the last lap progressed. But at least I was running free and out of trouble, and I was able to kick past him where I wanted to, on the final bend. I was absolutely flat out in the straight – I tried to drive again about forty metres out, and I knew there was just nothing more there. I didn't dare look to see what was happening behind me, and the anxiety over the last twenty metres was unbearable.

And then I was through the finish. The feeling was extraordinary; normally the last thing I would do would be to go down on my knees on the track – but the relief was overpowering, and so was the thought, just for a moment, of 'Thank God that's over. Never again!'

Perhaps it wasn't until I looked back later that I realised how great the pressure had been, and how great the release when it was all over. A few days after I got home to Sheffield I was out on one of my usual runs in the country when suddenly I came to a dead stop. I just stood there thinking, for the first time, I suppose, of what would have happened if I had lost both races. It didn't bear thinking about.

It had taken only seven short months of 1980 – the build-up, the detailed preparation, the dozens of press and television and radio interviews, the political wrangles, the uncertainty, the irresistible rising tension, the last-minute doubts, the constant wish that it could all be over. Then came the action at last, the dreadful disappointment of a silver medal instead of a gold, and the self-reproach at running such an appalling race. Finally the recovery, the new confidence, the victory, the glorious, absurd fuss . . . and then the release of tension, and the inevitable psychological let-down until normal life took over again. That was the Olympic Games.

It will always remain a unique experience in my life, as it must do in the lives of many thousands of athletes from the past, and since Moscow I have looked back with much more curiosity, and perhaps with rather more understanding, to the great competitors of earlier days. Had they, I wondered, encountered the same pressures as we had? Had they revelled in the atmosphere of the Games, or had they been swept along on the Games' powerful wave, only to look back afterwards to realise how much their medal meant to them?

It was fascinating to speculate, after my own experiences, how some people had won titles and some had failed to win them, how all the talent and training had worked for some and had left others empty-handed. And how some of the greatest performers had influenced the very history of athletics by their performances under the Olympic spotlight.

These thoughts, from my own reading, my own memories and my conversations with some of the Olympians themselves, amount not so much to a chronological account of Olympic athletics, packaged neatly in four-year chunks, but rather a series of ideas that bind together various strands from the modern history of the Games: the all-conquering Finns, the black American sprinters, the pioneering women, the great Olympians who never won medals, and many more.

It is themes such as these which form the chapters of *The Olympians*. All have intrigued me over the years, and all stem from the incomparable fascination of the Olympic Games themselves.

Overpowering relief and unrestrained delight. Jurgen Straub gives his congratulations (*left*) **and the release of tension is almost tangible.**

THE IDEA OF THE GIFTED AMATEUR is a deeply attractive one. The idol who could play the game for the sake of the game, make his century at Lord's and then go back to teach Greek or make a House of Commons speech with his wind-blown hair restored to its Corinthian perfection, was the very model of Edwardian excellence.

This idealistic blueprint for the ideal human being helped to develop an even more attractive theory – that sport played by such selfless amateurs was itself a force for good in the world, an example to the inhabitants of lesser nations, a positive contribution to world peace, and so on. It was an ideal deeply embedded in the Olympic spirit, and there is no doubt that on a personal level the Games, like all well organised sporting occasions, promoted friendly rivalry and companionship that took no account of national boundaries.

Moreover, in its first half-century the Games did produce an attractive number of young competitors who, on the surface, did just what the Olympic idealists dreamed they would. They took a little time off their preparations for running the world – from their studies as teachers or doctors or businessmen or missionaries – they thrilled the crowds and enjoyed the keen contest ... and then went back to fulfil their destiny.

It all seemed so informal, so effortless.

Ted Flack lived up to the ideal. He left Australia in the mid-1890s, taking time away from the family firm of Davey, Flack and Co. to gain some experience of accountancy in England. In 1892 he had helped to found Melbourne Hare and Hounds, and in London he joined three running clubs, and ran a lot in his spare time. No Australian team was entered for the first Olympic Games in Athens, but Ted Flack travelled as a private citizen having taken a month off work, reached Greece by train and boat, and was recommended a cheap hotel by the British Consul in Athens. He wandered round the city as a tourist, was a little disappointed at the somewhat bat-

The natural and the sheer professional: Eric Liddell's flowing strength (*left*) **contrasted with the finely honed technique of Harold Abrahams.**

tered appearance of the stadium and felt, in his amateur way, that it was hardly in keeping with these new Games that people should actually have to be charged to watch them.

When the Games started, he moved out of his hotel to share a flat with an English hammer-thrower, George Stuart Robertson; no hammer event had been included in the Games, so Robertson had cheerfully entered for the discus and the weight instead. Ted Flack did not really expect to do very well, and he had developed a bit of a cold in Athens. But he won his heat of the 800 metres in a slow time on the crazy hairpin bends of the old Athens stadium, and felt satisfied enough.

Between the two rounds of the 800 metres they had organised the final of the 1500 metres; and to the rejoicing of the British holidaymakers in the stadium Flack won it from the fancied American Arthur Blake. Two days later he won his second final, the 800 metres, then he got on a horse-bus to drive to Marathon on the coast, a roundabout, uncomfortable four-hour journey. The Greeks had been setting great store by the showpiece of their Games, and Ted Flack wanted to be a part of it. He stayed the night at the home of a hospitable Greek, and then prepared to run back to Athens in the first marathon race of all.

He had never run so far in his life before (nor, to be fair, had the Frenchman or the Americans, though the Greeks had been training hard at it for months). After ten of the 40 kilometres he found himself in second place; at 25 kilometres he was still second, and the chasers, including Arthur Blake, had fallen away; at 30 kilometres he strode past the Frenchman Lermusiaux into the lead. At 35 kilometres, slowed almost to a walk and staggering from side to side, he collapsed, and a Greek strode by into the lead.

The ambulance drove him fast back to the stadium, where Prince Nicholas of Greece ordered him an egg beaten in brandy; and he had recovered sufficiently to watch in wonder as the 70,000 crowd, packing the cigar-shaped stadium solid, roared a welcome to their own man.

The Athenians gloried in their victory, but they admired, too, the modest Australian who had twice been crowned with the victor's olive wreath, and who had come so close to glory on the dusty roads from Marathon. After a week of parties and dinners and sightseeing and general lionisation Ted Flack took his train back to London, finished his spell of accountancy there, and returned to Melbourne to lead the family firm to profit and success.

The early years of the Games are full of such stories, not always of victory and hero-worship but of ease and friendship and hospitality; almost, at times, of a long-forgotten, child-like innocence. Philip Noel-Baker, who perhaps more than any Briton revelled for his entire long life in his belief in the essential excellence of the Olympic spirit, looked back with misty eyes to his first Games, at Stockholm in 1912.

With Arnold Strode-Jackson, the Oxford University miler, he dined at the Opera Café on their second night in Stockholm, and not surprisingly made

such a hash of reading the Swedish menu that instead of being served with a modest table d'hôte they were confronted with two waiters bearing vast silver trays stacked with the largest lobsters they had ever seen. The athletes were rescued by a Swedish diner and his wife sitting at a nearby table who recognised their team blazers, apologised for the mix-up on behalf of all their fellow-countrymen, bought them each a steak, and every evening for the rest of the Games drove them out into the cool of the Swedish countryside for dinner at a lakeside restaurant.

For Noel-Baker it was the start of a love affair with the Olympic movement that lasted till his death seventy years later. For Strode-Jackson it was the idyllic background to a week in which he had to adapt to the conventional conditions of the Stockholm stadium after years of running at Iffley Road, Oxford – where the track was not only 586 yards and 2 feet round (three to a mile) but, by some strange tradition that the university

shared with Cambridge, was run clockwise. He did so to such effect that, with some expert pacing from his companion Noel-Baker in the early laps, he outsmarted and outsprinted the formidable American team to win a magnificent 1500 metres gold medal.

When the Games resumed after the First World War some of the illusions of leisured ease were still there – athletes, for example, still stayed at hotels dotted round the host city, and frequently had to scramble for taxis to get to their heats on time – but even for the true amateurs of the day competition had become

Paris defeat (*below*): **Liddell (third from left) and Abrahams (second from right) beaten at 200 metres by Scholz and the leaping Paddock. Paris victory** (*right*): **Abrahams dips in the 100 metres to beat Scholz (arms raised in top picture) and the black-vested Arthur Porritt.**

Lord Burghley, hurdles victor at Amsterdam and master administrator. *Opposite:* **Jack Lovelock, university hopeful (running with fellow-Oxonian Jerry Cornes) and Berlin hero.**

fierce, and training necessarily harder and more systematic.

It was this sense of change which, more than fifty years later, was encapsulated with great effect in the film *Chariots of Fire*, which set against each other the contrasting paths of two Britons to gold medals at the Paris Games of 1924. Harold Abrahams and Eric Liddell were both undisputed amateurs, both highly talented sprinters, both set on success at the Games.

Abrahams could be described as the new amateur, full of ambition, aware of the task ahead of him and prepared to go to almost any lengths to attain his maximum potential. He went to Antwerp in 1920 as a Cambridge undergraduate of distinct promise, but failed to reach the final of the 100 metres. He employed his own coach, the legendary Sam Mussabini, to prepare him for the 1924 campaign, and spent months refining his sprinting technique – his arm movement, his start, his finishing dip. It was a single-minded pursuit of excellence which is familiar to a top-class athlete today, but which was certainly something of an exception in the regime of a middle-class trainee barrister in the 1920s. In Paris the seemingly all-powerful American squad (there were four of them in the six-man 100 metre final) could not match Abrahams's preparation and timing, and Abrahams won his gold medal.

Eric Liddell, on the other hand, really was the personification of the amateur ideal – large as life and almost too good to be true. He was the son of a Scottish missionary, and was himself to follow his father to a calling in China, ruled all his life by an unfailing religious faith. His early sporting mark was made as a rugby player, and he was capped seven times as a wing three-quarter for Scotland. When he retired from the game to concentrate on athletics he quickly established himself as the fastest runner Britain had ever seen – certainly faster than Abrahams (though the two never ran against each other on the track before the Paris Games) and certainly Britain's choice to take on the Americans in the Olympics.

His talent was such that he seemed to thrive on the few informal and somewhat sketchy training sessions he managed to fit in each week alongside his academic studies and his Scotland-wide preaching engagements. His commitment to gold in Paris, while genuine, was less than all-consuming, and when the programme for the Olympics athletic competitions was announced, Liddell quietly but unshakably declined to run in either the 100 metres, the 4 × 100 metres relay or the 4 × 400 metres relay, because all of them involved heats to be run on a Sunday. True, once more, to the idealists' dreams, he changed events, won a bronze medal in the 200 metres and, by an unprecedented display of near-suicidal front-running, won the 400 metres final by a good five metres. It was a near-perfect plot for a work of schoolboy fiction, the stuff that evangelical sermons were made of, and it probably marked a watershed in amateur sport.

If the commitment of an athlete like Abrahams was slightly alien to the British sporting tradition, it was already deeply ingrained in the United States. At Oxford and Cambridge and Edinburgh you still shook hands with the other chaps before and after the race, win or lose. In the dozens of universities blooming across the United States commitment was everything, and winning, despite Baron de Coubertin's ethic, the only reason for taking part. Since the last decade of the nineteenth century the football coach had been a major force on the staff of any college, and for the reputation of that college his students were expected to win games. Since America's early successes at the Olympic Games, many colleges had added an athletics coaching team to their staff and built running tracks round their stadiums. The prestige of producing a world record breaker or an inter-collegiate athletic champion had become every bit as important as that of producing an All-American quarterback.

The coaching was well conceived, systematic and well paid – and remained the best overall system for producing amateur athletes until well after the Second World War. Inter-college rivalry was intense, and in itself probably accounted for much of the commitment of the best American champions.

In 1932, when the Games came to the American continent for the first time since 1904, a dozen American track and field successes bore witness to this commitment, none more so than the 400 metres where two outstanding runners and their followers split the nation's loyalties in two. Ben Eastman, from Stanford University on the West Coast, made the first play by breaking the world record by a full second four months before the Games. He was immediately established as odds-on favourite for the gold medal.

Then, twice in a fortnight in July, both times on his own territory in Cali-

Triumph in Berlin: Lovelock's crucial break 300 metres from home steals three vital strides from Cunningham and Beccali. Off the final bend he is still comfortable in a decisive lead; by the tape (*right*) the order is the same and the victory emphatic.

fornia, he was beaten by Bill Carr, an Easterner from Pennsylvania University. The confrontation was all the more fascinating as their respective coaches were long-standing rivals, and between them Eastman and Carr staged a classic Olympic final, effectively creating a race separate from that of the other finalists. The bespectacled Eastman, drawn favourably inside his rival, held a marginal lead until the final straight and then Carr, whose pace judgment on the outside had been masterly, drove past to win by a couple of yards in a new world record. No-one else finished within a second of them.

The triumphant Carr anchored the Americans to another world record and the gold medal in the long relay later in the week, comfortably beating a team more representative of the old and still flourishing Oxbridge tradition. The Britons did well enough to set a European record, and their second-change runner that day could be said to have shared with Liddell and Abrahams the task of shaping British athletics awareness in its crucial transformation period. Abrahams was a middle-class professional with a professional's approach to athletics and to life; Liddell was a muscular Christian with a love of God and his

fellow man and, almost incidentally, of winning rugby matches and running races. David Burghley, son, heir and later successor to the Marquess of Exeter, was a rich aristocrat utterly steeped in athletics. He competed in three Games, just qualifying for a high hurdles place in Paris, majestically winning the 400 metres hurdles title in Amsterdam, and reaching both hurdles finals, as well as winning his relay silver medal, in Los Angeles. While Abrahams channelled his energies and his directness back into the sport through journalism and broadcasting and, eventually, administration, and Liddell left it all behind cheerfully enough to spread the gospel in the Far East, Burghley was to be at the forefront of athletics all his life.

Britain loved nothing more, it seemed, than a lord a-leaping, and hardly had he stopped hurdling than he became president of the Amateur Athletic Association. Soon after peace had returned in the mid-1940s he was organising his own Olympic Games as mastermind to the 1948 Games in battle-scarred London. At the end of the war, too, he had become President of the International Amateur Athletic Federation, a post which he held till after his seventieth birthday, presiding over more change in the sport at home and abroad than he can possibly have conceived as he trained (clockwise, of course) round the Cambridge track at Fenners in the early 1920s.

By the Second World War, though, the 'classic' amateur athletics tradition, at the highest level at least, was in an inevitable decline. But it did not depart without a glorious flourish in Berlin in 1936, when a dedicated medical student devoted himself, just for a short and preordained period, to producing athletic perfection.

Jack Lovelock, curly-haired, fresh-faced, introspective, had come to Oxford as a Rhodes Scholar from New Zealand, and had been lucky to enjoy a friendship and a rivalry with Jerry Cornes, then President of the Oxford athletics club and already established as an international athlete of standing. Between them they lifted the university's athletics to new heights of excellence, and both were selected for the Los Angeles Games

in 1932, Cornes for Britain, Lovelock for New Zealand. Cornes's success in winning a silver medal in the 1500 metres behind the Italian Luigi Beccali was tempered by his friend's disappointment at his own seventh place in the final. Lovelock, though, had plenty of time left as a student – a medical degree is a long one, and a long hospital training follows it – so he returned to his studies and his university athletics with determination still intact.

Lovelock was an obsessively analytical athlete. He examined his own performances day by day as a doctor might study a patient, and his voluminous notebooks revealed honesty, awareness, sternness at failure and, occasionally, satisfaction at progress. By 1934 he was accepted as the best miler in the Empire, winning that title by beating Cornes and the emerging Sydney Wooderson with some ease. By the summer of 1935 he had beaten the world record holder Glenn Cunningham and the other American giant Bill Bonthron in a much-vaunted 'Mile of the Century' at Princeton. The only cloud on his pre-Olympic horizon was some late-season defeats by Wooderson, whose last-lap kick had become the most formidable in the world, and the self-doubt inflicted by his own merciless notes.

His meticulous preparation for the Berlin Games began late in 1935 with a self-enforced lay-off after the hectic travel of the previous season. He was now working at St Mary's Hospital; he swam occasionally, and walked a bit, but took part in none of the usual road relays or cross-country meetings. He broke his rule once to the extent of donning boxing gloves to win the featherweight title at the inter-hospital championships, but he did not participate in any running competition until late April. Even when the season began he avoided meeting Cornes or Wooderson in the British Games, and made no bid to gain selection for the AAA teams.

It was at this time that a serious doubt, fostered by his long absence from the tack and by the memory of his 1935 defeats by Wooderson, began to plague him. Had he really lost his old finishing speed? And, if so, should he not prepare as well for the 5000 metres? Incredibly,

just two months before Berlin, he decided that he would have to. He embarked on the most intensive training of his career; his distance running in the spring had been invaluable as background for a possible tilt at the 5000 metres, but he was also determined to recapture all the speed he could. He ran intervals, he ran long speed-endurance trials, he practised pace-judgment, he deliberately put on weight – measuring his progress all the time in his notebooks.

Even in Berlin he was not sure which title to go for. The New Zealand selectors had entered him for both races. He and Jerry Cornes qualified together with ease in a slow heat for the 1500 metres. Lovelock put on his tracksuit, picked up his running number for the 5000 metres heats which were due the following day – the same day as the 1500 metres final – and went off to decide which one to scratch from.

He ran, of course, in the 1500 metres. He went for it with the reassuring knowledge that an injured Wooderson had failed to qualify for the final, and he went with a plan to use his new-found strength to surprise and escape from the field in the early stages of the final lap and hold on till the finish.

And that precisely is what he did, breaking clear of Cunningham, the champion Beccali and a briefly challenging Swede at 300 metres, completing the last lap in 56 seconds, breaking a chunk off the old world record and winning New Zealand's first Olympic athletics gold medal. It elicited from Harold Abrahams, dedicated amateur and by now dedicated broadcaster, the least objective athletics commentary by an Englishman that can ever have been recorded for posterity:

'Cunningham still leading,' he broadcast, voice rising with every sentence. 'Lovelock just behind him, just the same position he had out in America a year ago. Let's hope the result's going to be the same . . .

'Lovelock's running superbly now. Come on, Jack . . .

'Three hundred metres to go – Lovelock leads. Three hundred metres to go. Lovelock. Cunningham leading – no, no, Lovelock leads by three yards . . .

'Cunningham's fighting hard, Beccali coming up to his shoulder. Lovelock leads. Lovelock! Lovelock!

'Come on, Jack, a hundred yards to go. Come on, Jack. My God, he's done it. *Jack! Come on!*

'Lovelock wins! Five yards, six yards. He wins, he's won. Hurrah!'

In his notebook that night Lovelock penned his own verdict on the Berlin

1500 metres – precise, clinical, frank, unselfconscious, a verdict that allows no argument from us even after nearly fifty years: 'It was the most perfectly executed race of my career.'

Jack Lovelock had, after much heart-searching, been able to blend the ideals of an amateur dedicated to running with the ideals of a student dedicated to his chosen profession. After the War such a

Iffley Road, Oxford, 1954. One of the last great days of the old amateur tradition: Chris Brasher leads Roger Bannister and Chris Chataway through the first lap on the way to Bannister's historic four-minute mile.

blend became rare, almost an impossibility. Britain still bred its heroes who combined the two with talent – athletes like Roger Bannister, for example, four-minute mile legend and doctor, or Chris Chataway, White City conqueror of Vladimir Kuts and budding politician.

But neither of these could harness their talents to an Olympic medal of any colour – the part-time Olympian was no longer a possibility. This fact was recognised by their colleague and university contemporary Chris Brasher who, with astute calculation, set aside two years of his life and postponed any real thoughts of a career in the attempt to win an Olympic title at an unfashionable event ... and he succeeded.

This is not to belittle the old Olympic ideals. The decline of 'pure' amateurism does not in itself imply a decline in sportsmanship. When Brasher faced disqualification after his runaway victory in the Melbourne steeplechase it was not the athletes who had objected; indeed, the fourth man home, Heinz Laufer, made it clear that he would in no circumstances accept a medal if Brasher's disqualification stood. The code among runners is still an honourable one.

Nevertheless, the hankering after the old amateur ideals is still there. The old school still looks askance at advertisements on vests, salutes of victory to the television cameras, laps of honour, athletics scholarships and the scrambling among agents to sign up stars for post-Olympic meetings. But an athlete's life is short, and as an ex-athlete he commands little attention. As an active participant his entertainment value is high, and once every four years it's unrivalled. It takes many years of hard, continuous work to get anywhere near an Olympic final, let alone to win it, and sport is no longer for the men and women who can afford the luxury of full-time sport for sport's sake.

Remember Spiridon Louis, winner of that first marathon in the days of ideals and pure amateurism and the new-born Olympic spirit. For his victory he got more than the kisses of a Greek prince and a laurel wreath: among the other things that a Greek victor had been promised were free haircuts, free transport and free groceries for life.

PAAVO NURMI

Two Finnish
masters: Lasse
Viren of the
1970s, Paavo
Nurmi of the
1920s.

NO COUNTRY HAS BECOME MORE PASSIONATELY ENTWINED with the Olympic Games than Finland, which makes it rather odd that the most exciting athletics moment for the Finns since the Second World War came not in an Olympic Games but in the less intense arena of the European Championships.

It happened, though, in Helsinki, in front of the most knowledgeable crowd of athletics fans in the world, and it signalled a rebirth of Finnish long-distance running that the Finns had been searching and praying for since the late 1930s.

That hero of 1971 was Juha Vaatainen, an unlikely-looking champion – short, almost bald, sporting a pair of blond mutton-chop whiskers. He was something of an enigma to the Finns, too. He was very much a loner, which in itself is far from rare in Finland, but he was also inclined to be at odds with authority, and had the singular honour in his year of triumph to be voted, in a national poll, both the Most Popular Finn and the Most Unlikeable Finn at one and the same time.

In the Helsinki Olympic Stadium on 10 August 1971, Vaatainen blazed round the final lap of the 10,000 metres final to destroy Jurgen Haase and the rest of a world-class field and take the title amid a tumult which, for anyone who has never witnessed at first hand a stadium packed with rejoicing Finns, can only be imagined.

The tumult redoubled four days later when he once again accelerated away from the pack in the 5000 metres final to give Finland the double distance gold. It was 'only' a European Championship, to be sure, but the delirious Finns were convinced that the long wait was over . . .

It had, indeed, been a long wait; no gold medals on the track since 1936, not even in Finland's own Olympic Games of 1952. And this in a country whose middle- and long-distance runners had been invincible for two decades and more.

The new torchbearer: Juha Vaatainen (738) tracks David Bedford in the European 10,000 metres. *Opposite:* **the pioneer, Hannes Kolehmainen, and his duel with Jean Bouin at Stockholm.**

It is an unusual nation to have made such an impact on athletics history. It has, so the Finns themselves tell us, the shortest and most beautiful summer in the world. This may well be so; summers among the forests and hills of the wild north are certainly a runner's paradise. But Finland also has the coldest, longest and most brutal of winters. Breath freezes, training means running on icy roads or drifting snow, and most Finns take what comfort they can in thick-walled houses and strong alcohol.

Finland had no 19th-century tradition of running, and while athletic sports were gaining popularity in Britain and other parts of the continent the Finns remained happier with gymnastics. Only in the army did running races tend to be organised, and as the Finnish army in those days was run by authoritarian Russian officers, it is likely that a certain

amount of needle entered the contests. There was certainly no interest in distance running until the late 1880s, when a British professional runner called Dibbles ran a demonstration race in Helsinki – six miles in 33 minutes, running a straight 100 metre course back and forth, stopping and turning at each end. The public took to him (though not, mercifully, to his choice of track) and the Finns began running.

Even so, no runners travelled from Finland to any of the first three Olympic Games. The tales filtering back from the Games did reach receptive ears, however, and after a marathon had been organised in Helsinki in 1906, and the winner had subsequently represented Finland in 'Dorando's Marathon' at the 1908 London Games – he came a respectable 11th – Finland gradually went Olympic crazy. To prove it, within four years they had produced the best runner in the world. Within a dozen years they had followed this up by producing the greatest distance competitor of all time, and also by laying the foundations of a national stable of runners who were to dominate world athletics for a decade and a half.

The first great Finnish Olympian, smiling Hannes Kolehmainen, was the youngest of three hard-working, hard-running brothers, all of whom could have made Olympic history had their lives taken a different turn. Viljami Kolehmainen, the eldest, left for America, turned professional, changed his first name to the more manageable Willie, and, running the whole race on a track, became the first man to break two-and-a-half hours for the marathon. Tatu, the other brother, set world best times for 20 kilometres and 25 kilometres.

Hannes himself took the Stockholm Olympics by storm. He won the 10,000 metres with a display of front running that had destroyed the rest of the field by half way; he won the cross country with ease; he set a world record for the 3000 metres in a team race. And he crowned the week with victory in the 5000 metres, one of the great races in Olympic history,

Nurmi the machine, pictured shortly before his retirement. *Right:* **Nurmi the legend, carrying the Olympic flame into the Helsinki stadium in 1952.**

A diffident young Nurmi (*left*) **with his French rival Joseph Guillemot at Antwerp, and** (*below*) **characteristically shadowing his Finnish rival Ville Ritola in Amsterdam.**

which provided the precedent for a dozen memorable Olympic 5000 metre finals, and which saw the pride of Finland beat the pride of France, Jean Bouin, by mere inches in a two-man battle which kept the participants and spectators guessing until literally the last second, and which broke the existing world record by nearly half a minute.

In 1912 Kolehmainen and the other Finns ran under the Russian flag; with the Bolshevik revolution in Russia, and after a sharp civil war at home, Finland won its independence and a fierce national pride added even more fuel to its hungry runners. By the Antwerp Games of 1920 the great Kolehmainen was still good enough to win the marathon in the fastest time recorded to date by an amateur, but eyes were now turning from smiling Hannes to the positively unsmiling twenty-three-year-old crown prince, Paavo Nurmi.

The single-mindedness that was to in-furiate officials and teammates alike for nearly fifteen years seems to have been fully formed at the astonishingly early age of twelve, when young Paavo decided to train 'easily and steadily for five years, then add quality and quantity'. For years he attempted nothing more than endurance training in the forests. By the time he was nineteen he was taking long early-morning walks (an integral part of most Finnish runners' programmes, something the old, retired Nurmi, looking back on his career, considered his greatest mistake), running some short sprints after work, running distance in the forests before dinner, and finishing off the day 'jumping and throwing his arms all round the house'. Stretching and flexibility exercises had arrived!

In 1919 he began his eighteen months' military service, found more time to train, and beat the ageing Tatu Kolehmainen in a 10,000 metres race. The next year he was a certainty for the Finnish Olympic team, and his first Olympic final in Antwerp pitted Finland with France as it had in 1912. Bouin had been killed in the war, and Joseph Guillemot was the new French hope for the 5000 metres. The young Nurmi took the hare's role, and despite reaching the half distance in 7 min 11 sec he began to tire. Guillemot closed the gap, took the lead and won by five seconds. France had gained her revenge for the Stockholm defeat. It was eight years before Nurmi was to be beaten in an Olympic race again.

A few days later, in the Antwerp 10,000 metres, he turned the tables on Guillemot by allowing the Frenchman to set the pace and outsprinting him on the last lap; Guillemot injured himself in the cross-country, and Nurmi won with ease, leading the Finnish runners to the team title as well. That meant a total of three golds and one silver for Paavo Nurmi.

From that week in Antwerp the legend grew. Nurmi the invincible, Nurmi the machine, Nurmi the silent, Nurmi the man with the stopwatch who hurled it on to the infield at the start of the blistering last lap. By 1924 Nurmi had added speed to his phenomenal endurance and captured the world 1500 metre

and mile records. He had become something of a god to the Finns and, dare it be said, something of an embarrassment to the Finnish officials.

Finland had a squad of runners absolutely supreme. Just as today *any* squad picked from America's top ten sprinters could be expected to take a major haul of the medals at an international championship, so in the 1920s any one of four or five Finns could be expected to lead the field home in any distance race in the Olympic Games. The trouble was that Nurmi wanted – and was good enough – to win them all.

The Finnish Olympic Committee, having paid for Ville Ritola to sail back from his home in America and train in Europe for the Paris Games, deprived Nurmi of a gold medal by the simple expedient of withdrawing him from the 10,000 metres altogether, leaving the title to Ritola for the taking. The Finnish public was bewildered, Nurmi's fury at being deprived of a chance to defend his Olympic title can only be guessed at (press conferences to dwell on such controversies were less common in 1924), and no-one has yet positively confirmed the story that while Ritola was winning his title Nurmi was out on a nearby track with his stopwatch running his own 10,000 metres – forty seconds faster. It is a measure of Nurmi's reputation that everybody was, and still is, inclined to believe such a preposterous tale.

Where the Finns succeeded in spreading the medal hoard out a bit, the Paris organisers singularly failed. Their apparent master-stroke was to arrange the 1500 metres and 5000 metres finals within an hour of each other. Nurmi's response came in two parts. The first, at a 'general rehearsal' for the Games, was to win a 1500 metre race in a new world record and then, fifty-five minutes later, win a 5000 metre race in a new world record. The second was to do precisely the same thing (albeit in slightly slower times) in Paris, and follow this by beating Ritola and the rest of the field in the cross country. This last was held on the hottest day in Olympic history; only fif-

Nurmi's greatest day, Paris 1924. An hour earlier he had won the 1500 metres. Now, on the inside lane, he starts his bid for the 5000 metres.

And then came the war, two brave, sapping and ultimately disastrous campaigns against the Russians and, with the image of Nurmi fading fast, a famine on the track. And what a famine: between 1912 and 1936 Finland's track athletes had won twenty-four gold medals (including those for team races). From London in 1948 to Mexico City in 1968, six Games in all, Finland's runners won just two medals, both bronze, one in the marathon and one in the 400 metres (the latter was awarded for a dead-heat third place in Melbourne; it remains the only medal of any sort won by a Finn in a flat race shorter than 1500 metres).

The pride of the nation was dented badly. In 1952, when the Olympic

Lauri Lehtinen, successor to Nurmi and Ritola as 5000 metres champion, Los Angeles, 1932.

teen of the thirty-eight starters were still standing at the end, and the third Finn, Liimatainen, was so exhausted that he took a wrong turning, then collapsed twice, and had to be coaxed over the line on his knees so that Finland could win the team gold medal. With another gold in the 3000 metres team race, Nurmi went home with an unprecedented and unequalled five from Paris; and four years later he brought his grand total to nine when, back with Ritola in the 10,000 metres, he rubbed in his message by beating his fellow-countryman into second place.

By now, though, there were signs that his legs had lost some of their power. He fell heavily in the heats of the steeplechase, and the following day Ritola had the measure of him in the 5000 metres final. In the steeplechase final a tired Nurmi seemed content to lead the pack home in second place, surrendering the gold medal to a much more sophisticated steeplechaser, his compatriot Loukola. It was Nurmi's last Olympic race, and

Clean sweep: Iso-Hollo (3rd), Askola (2nd) and the eventual winner Salminen lead the 10,000 metres field in Berlin.

like his first, eight years before, it won him a silver medal. He kept running for another four years until, shortly before the Los Angeles Games of 1932, he was declared a professional and banned from the marathon which no-one expected him to lose. Ritola retired after the 1928 Games, a superb runner by any standards, and a legend himself had not the shadow of Nurmi been so colossal.

The legacy of Kolehmainen was still burning brightly in Finland. Nurmi might have gone, but still there was Volmari Iso-Hollo to win the steeplechase in Los Angeles and again in Berlin; there was an unbroken run of victories in the 5000 metres, Nurmi and Ritola being followed by Lehtinen in 1932 and Höckert in 1936; there was the 10,000 metres in 1936, when Finland swept the medals board through Salminen, Askola and Iso-Hollo; and then....

Finns of the golden era *(above)*; Ville Ritola leads Paavo Nurmi and the Swede Edvin Wide in the Amsterdam 10,000 metres. Nurmi came home in front for his ninth and last Olympic gold medal; his career was commemorated by a statue in Helsinki *(top right)*.

Finn of the revival *(right)*: Pekka Vasala kicks away from Keino and New Zealand's Rod Dixon to an unexpected victory in the Munich 1500 metres.

Finland's modern master: Lasse Viren's double long-distance double turned back the clock to Finland's domination of the 1920s. Opposite page (*top*): Munich victory in the 5000 metres (*left*) ahead of Gammoudi and 10,000 metres (*right*) ahead of Puttemans. Opposite page (*below*): Montreal victory in the 5000 metres over Quax of New Zealand (691) and Hildenbrand of West Germany (428). Top: Montreal victory in the 10,000 metres, after a tussle with Portugal's Lopes and Britain's Brendan Foster (364). Right: defeat, his first on an Olympic track, in the 10,000 metres at Moscow, beaten by advancing age and the Ethiopians Kedir (178) and Yifter (191). The latter took the gold medal, Viren was fifth.

Emil Zatopek in 1948 – the arrival of a long-distance phenomenon.

Vladimir Kuts in 1956 – the hard-bitten heir to Zatopek's titles.

The new order: Lasse Viren leads Juha Vaatainen as Finland's running asserts its old authority.

Games came at last to Helsinki, the two fathers of the country's athletic greatness summoned from every Finn a roar of profound and unprecedented emotion as Paavo Nurmi carried the torch into the stadium and, having lit one flame, passed on the torch to Hannes Kolehmainen to light the other. But not a single gold medal for the Finns to revel in. Not even in the javelin, their other great traditional love, in which their athletes have won five Olympic titles since the First World War. Worse was to come. In the three Games between Melbourne and Munich no Finn even won through to an Olympic track final.

The transformation, when it came, was extraordinary. In the Sixties a number of foreign coaches had made what almost amounted to a pilgrimage to Finland – Igloi of Hungary, Lydiard of New Zealand, the former only for a few weeks, the latter on a ridiculously short contract in an attempt (doomed almost before it began) to find Finland some medal-winners for the Mexico Games of 1968. Neither produced immediate results, but both demonstrated the need for a reassessment of Finland's training methods, and both inspired athletes to previously unheard-of hard work, and coaches to provide the training schedules.

Once again the Finns were doing what Kolehmainen and Nurmi had done before – setting themselves single-mindedly at ambitious targets, prepared to work with every effort every week of the year, aiming to recapture what every Finn, athlete or not, considered his birthright – the reflected glory of Olympic gold.

When Vaatainen won his European double in 1971 it came as a shaft of light in the deepest gloom. In 1968 their distance runners had been so bad that only three had been selected to go to Mexico City: one was ill and didn't run, one dropped out of the marathon part-way through the race and the third, a young 1500-metre runner called Pekka Vasala, trailed in last in his first-round heat. Now, just four years later, as car-load after car-load of Finns, blue flags flying, sped down the autobahns to Munich, there was hope in the air again.

Vaatainen was the man they had come to cheer, but Vaatainen was to make way for a far greater athlete. As David Bedford dragged the 10,000 metre finalists through their third, painful mile, the American Frank Shorter bumped shoulders with a young Finn hardly known to the world six months before, Lasse Viren. Viren stumbled and fell, bringing down with him the Tunisian Mohamed Gammoudi. For Gammoudi it was the end of the race, but Viren was on his feet in no time; by the 5000 metre mark he was back with the leaders. By 6000 metres he had wrested the lead from Bedford; with 600 metres to go he launched his final attack, shed everyone but the Belgian Emiel Puttemans by the back straight of the final lap, and maintained full power down the home straight to break the world record and win Finland's first track gold medal for 36 years.

If Finland hailed a new master that day, they were beside themselves with rapture a week later; Viren wrapped the mantle of Nurmi even more securely round his shoulders by beating Gammoudi, Ian Stewart, the American Steve Prefontaine and Puttemans in a nerve-tingling 5000 metres final. And ten minutes after Viren had put his tracksuit back on, the unregarded outsider Pekka Vasala, four more years of relentless Lydiard-style training behind him, outsprinted Kip Keino to win the 1500 metres.

Four years later, after losing more races than he won – very often at the hands of Brendan Foster and usually without any great signs of urgency – Viren was back on the Olympic stage. With the whole of Finland chanting his name he proceeded to repeat himself. He won gold in the 10,000 metres (leaving Foster in third place) and gold in the 5000 metres, and enjoyed a good hour-and-a-half the next day when he

Viren's mastery at Munich: tracking the fancied American Prefontaine in the 5000 metres; leading Haro (169), Bedford and Puttemans (61) in the 10,000 metres.

threatened to do the impossible (or do a Zatopek, which by 1976 meant roughly the same thing) by winning the marathon as well. He came in fifth, and his greeting in the stadium was as warm as it had been for the winner.

If any of those races of Viren's still stirs the blood, it is that 5000 metres final – I would say that it's probably the most exciting race that I have ever seen. Viren doesn't say much at the best of times, and when he talks about his races it is usually in monosyllables, but the one thing I do remember him saying about that day in Montreal is that as the race progressed he became more and more terrified.

He had sat down and studied the field before the final, and he knew that he was going to have trouble outsprinting a lot of the runners in the field – Brendan Foster, Dick Quax and Rod Dixon were all fast finishers. And whenever he looked round during those twelve-and-a-half laps, there was what he called a black shadow at his shoulder. It might have been Dixon, it might have been Quax, but every time there was a New Zealand vest waiting, he felt, to pounce.

Viren's commitment was both courageous and brilliant. From 600 metres out he systematically wound up the pace so that each successive 100 metres was faster than the one before. It killed them all. The fast men who went into the final lap confident of a sprint at the finish found that there was no sprint left in them; and it was Viren, perhaps the slowest 100 metre runner in the top half of the field, with the fear ever-present that someone or other was still going to get past him in the last fifty metres, who outwitted them all to the tape. It was a tremendous display of bravery, and the Finns had provided the Games with yet another super-hero.

The question still remains. Why has this small nation become such an important part of the history of the Olympic Games? Is it something in their harsh geography, their impenetrable language or some stark philosophy of physical self-denial?

Finland's glory at Munich: Pekka Vasala sweeps off the final bend past Keino, and strides away to the 1500 metres finish.

Many western nations have their strong athletic traditions. France and Belgium have had their long-distance men, Italy her sprinters, Great Britain her middle-distance record-breakers. All have their idols, their occasional and ecstatically received gold medals, their more frequent gallant but vain attempts lower down the field. None, though, with all their tradition and their human resources, has the sheer will to win that characterises Finland. The Finns themselves ascribe it to something they call *sisu*, some combination of pride and stubbornness and guts. To a Finn with more than his fair share of *sisu*, all concepts but winning seem to disappear, all temptation to compromise is resisted, and he becomes twice the competitor, twice the opponent.

I say 'he' advisedly. The deeply conservative nature of Finnish society throughout most of this century has given its women a far slower start in athletic achievement than most of the rest of Europe. To date Finland's women have won just a single Olympic medal – a silver in their beloved javelin in 1948. Emancipation has arrived belatedly, though, and Finnish women won a singular honour in 1981 when Pirjo Häggman, their 400 metre runner who came tantalisingly close to a medal at Montreal, and who has consistently lobbied for wider sporting facilities throughout Finland for men and women alike, became the first women to be elected to full membership of the International Olympic Committee. If this social change brings *sisu* with it to Finnish women, too, and the javelin accomplishments of Tiina Lillak suggest that it might well have done so, the East Germans could be in for something of a fright.

In the lean years, *sisu* will bring the Finns Olympic success from unexpected quarters. Kaarlo Maaninka's silver medal behind Yifter in the Moscow 10,000 metres, achieved against opponents with far superior qualifications, was such a success, drawn painfully from him by effort and pride and a total refusal to be beaten. Or had he, as he later claimed in a sensational revelation to the press, been blood-doped? Perhaps he had, and his coach Jouko Elevaara

The greatest victory? The strain shows as Viren leads the field in the Montreal 5000 metres (*left*). **It shows even more on the faces of Quax (691), Hildenbrand (420) and the fourth-placed Dixon as Viren races home for his fourth Olympic gold medal.**

chilled the blood more than a little by responding 'As long as you're still alive for the victory ceremony, you should get your reward; there's no room for ethics in sport any more.' If this was more than idle rhetoric, if Maaninka's claim is more than attention-seeking boast, we have come painfully close to the boundary between sport and war, where athletes become cannon fodder and coaches are defending a political ideal rather than attacking a sporting target. Perhaps the answer is that the Finnish temperament has always been closer to this boundary than that of the rest of us. But it would be a tragedy if their appreciation of courage and skill and talent and dedication, and the pleasure it has given to so many

people, should lose all sense of proportion.

That said, Olympic success means more to a Finn than to any other citizen of any other country in the world. A new generation of runners is already in the background, working with a single-minded, self-denying devotion to duty towards Olympic gold, with Kolehmainen and Nurmi and Viren looking over their shoulders. They know that there is no achievement – in art or science or literature or sport – that could make their fellow countrymen more proud of them. To those of us from a country where sporting success is greeted with a roar one day and all but forgotten the next, that is an awesome thought.

JESSE OWENS

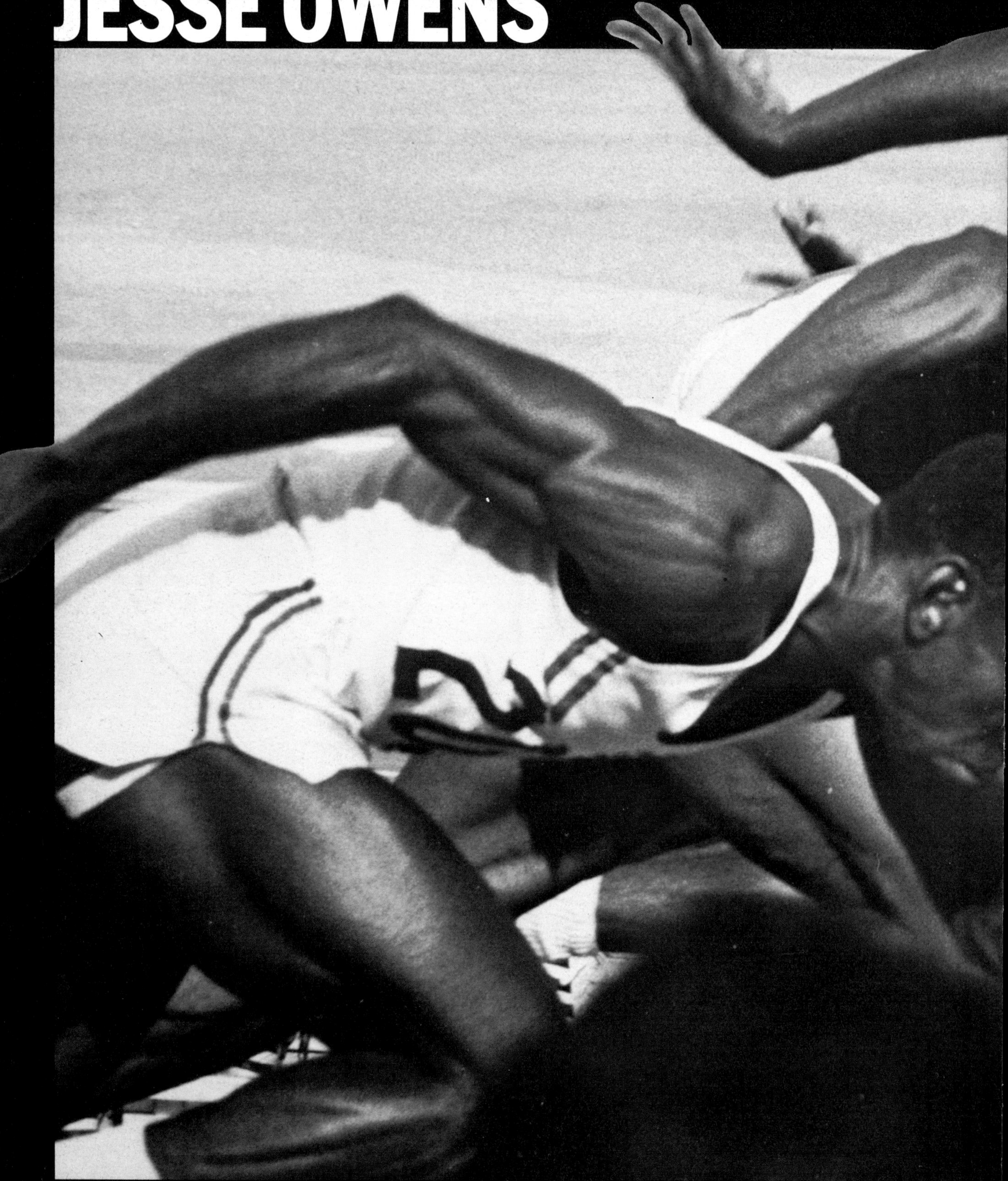

and the explosive breed

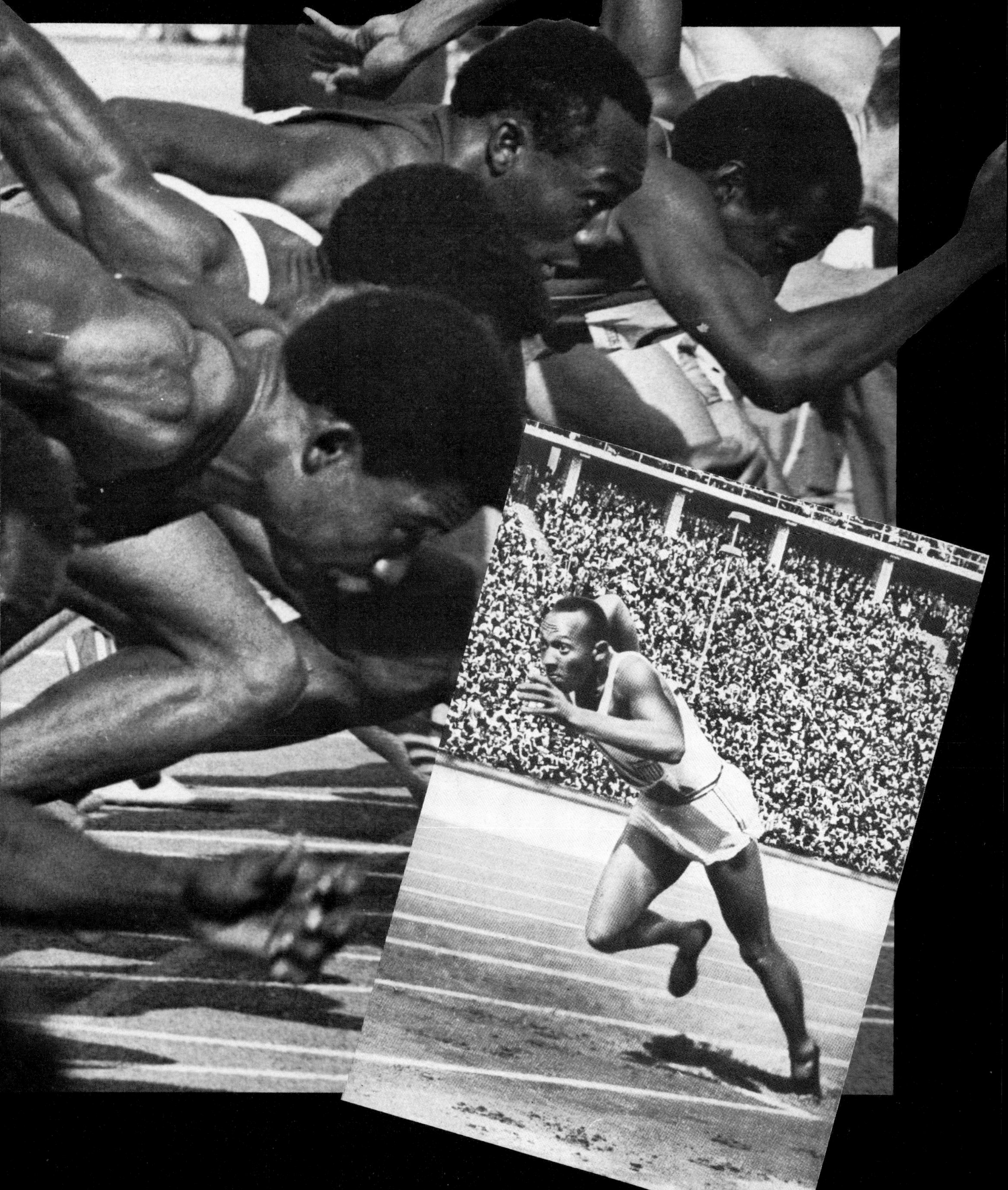

WE EXPECT BLACK AMERICANS TO BE FAST. We know, with a certainty that is tempered only by the facts, that they *always* win the big sprint titles. We group all black Americans together, whether they come from Ohio or California, New York or South Carolina, and we label them sprinters.

Smiles all round: Eddie Tolan, double sprint gold medallist in 1932; Jesse Owens, focus of all attention in 1936.

In a way we are right. Since Eddie Tolan stormed home to win both Los Angeles sprints in 1932 it has been something of a surprise, and something of a cause for American heart-searching, if they have not proved themselves dominant in the speed events. But their identification with speed has made more impact even than that; indeed, the rise of the black American athlete has been a more potent focus of political force than any other phenomenon in Olympic history.

And whoever emerges from elsewhere, from Europe, from Russia, from white America, to challenge this superiority for an Olympiad or two, the factors that made black United States sprinters the best in the world will still predominate: the American high school and college system with its attendant coaching facilities; the capitalist system's financial lure for the successful; the physical strength; and the extraordinary motivation in all Americans to *win*. It is surprising, but true, that no black American runner has won an Olympic gold medal since the War at any distance beyond 400 metres. Yet to win an Olympic sprint title it will always be necessary to beat a black American.

This explosive power had been in evidence well before the Los Angeles Games – most notably in the remarkable William de Hart Hubbard, who won the long jump title in Paris and the following year broke the world record for the 100 yards. But only in the late 1920s did black athletes begin to reach the high schools and colleges in sufficient numbers for the best of them to receive intensive coaching and provide opposition to the long tradition of white American sprinters. When they did arrive they came in numbers at the highest class, and they came in time to salvage a little lost pride for American athletics as a whole.

American sprinting had slipped away

No argument: Owens takes the Berlin 100 metres (*above*) **with a yard to spare from Metcalfe and** (*left*) **the 200 metres with silky, unhurried ease.**

badly in the late 1920s after their domination following the First World War. In 1920 Americans – white Americans, of course – took gold and silver in both the 100 and 200 metres, and the silver and bronze in the 110 metres hurdles behind a Canadian. In 1924 they repeated the 1920 act in the 200 metres and won the hurdles, though they lost the 100 metres title to Britain's Harold Abrahams. In 1928 it all went wrong: paraded in Amsterdam by their Olympic president Douglas MacArthur as the greatest ever to have left their shores, the Americans, against all prediction, failed to get a medal in either sprint, and were even pushed into the minor placings in the high hurdles, the last time *that* was to happen for forty-eight years.

For Los Angeles something had to be done, and the American revival came from two black runners who dominated all the pre-Games predictions – Eddie Tolan and Ralph Metcalfe. The former was a stocky, bespectacled, powerful Mid-Westerner who ran with a low-slung, short-striding action and had been in the top rank since 1929. Metcalfe, a tall and wide-shouldered Georgian, while still in his freshman year at university had come second behind Tolan in the national 220 yards championships, and in the Olympic trials the following year beat Tolan in both sprints, relegating the best of the white Americans, George Simpson, to third place in both.

Tolan won the Los Angeles 100 metres by inches from Metcalfe, and the 200 metres with ease from Simpson with Metcalfe in third place. Even so, old habits died hard in America, along with old prejudices; Tolan and Metcalfe were not selected for the sprint relay team, an all-white affair which justified (practically if not morally) the selectors' whim by winning the gold medal with some ease. The black American sprinters had arrived on the Olympic scene, however, and four years later the message was hammered home in the most dramatic circumstances possible.

Whether or not Jesse Owens remains the greatest black athlete of all time, whether he is the greatest Olympian of all time, cannot be proved one way or the other. One thing, however, is beyond

Berlin's finest contest: Owens's long-jumping could not be matched, but his friendship with the German runner-up Luz Long lasted until the latter's death in the War.

dispute: he won four Olympic gold medals in the space of ten days, which is a prodigious feat in itself. He did this in a supremely modest and good-natured way, in an arena which could have cowed any black man by the very implication of its grandeur, and he established incontestably the historical stature of the black athlete.

A lot has been written about what happened and what did not happen at those Nazi Games of 1936, much of it fanciful and composed well after the event, much of it inflated out of context. Whether or not Hitler really snubbed Jesse Owens after Owens's long-jump victory over

Luz Long is not important. The German was beaten by the American in one of the tensest and most enthralling field events competitions of all time, with Long finally going under only to a superb fifth-round jump by Owens.

Whatever Hitler thought, the victory was enough to infuriate Goebbels and his Nazi propaganda machine. In addition to the long jump, this boyish, unassuming black genius from Alabama took the 100 and 200 metres gold medals with ease (two black runners, Ralph Metcalfe and Mack Robinson won the respective silver medals) and blazed off his blocks in the 4 × 100 metres relay to give Metcalfe a 5-metre lead at the first change-over which the Americans never even looked like surrendering. The German command had described Owens, Metcalfe and the rest as 'Black mercenaries'. Not only had the mercenaries

trounced the Ayrians who were supposed to be superior to them, but they had captivated the German crowds in a way that no propaganda could have done; Owens himself remains the undoubted star of Leni Riefenstahl's brilliantly conceived official film of the Berlin Games, and he himself was received with warmth and due reverence by those Germans lucky enough to see him in action.

His feats in Berlin had been an incalculable psychological boost to the pride of the black American. Thirty years later, when black American athletes were again in the ascendancy, those looking for a more tangible *political* response to their people's achievements were to remember that when Jesse Owens returned to his hero's welcome in America's southern states he still had to sit in the segregated seats on the bus.

After the War the black sprinters carried on where they had been forced to leave off. Barney Ewell, who had come to prominence as early as 1937, was expected to fight out the London Olympic sprints with Mel Patton, a tall white Californian referred to with characteristic understatement in the U.S. press as 'The World's Fastest Human'. Both had reckoned without a specialist high-hurdler, Harrison Dillard, who had scraped into the team in third place in the American trials. Dillard only entered the 100 metres after hitting three hurdles and retiring from the event in which he had been expected to lead the United States team to its customary haul of medals (they still won all three, even without him). In a 100 metres final line-up of the highest class his nerve held better than anybody's, and even Ewell's tremendous kick in the final 20 metres failed to cancel out Dillard's superb start. Patton reasserted himself in the 200 metres, relegating Ewell once again to the minor placings, and Dillard and Ewell each picked up a gold medal in the sprint relay.

Much to the relief, no doubt, of the sprinters, Dillard went back to hurdling, and won the gold medal he so richly deserved four years later in Helsinki. Andy Stanfield led the American 1-2-3 in the 200 metres, but, significantly, it was a white American, Lindy Remigino, who emerged after a very long scrutiny of the photographs as winner of the 100 metres. And it was not until Tokyo, twelve years later, that the next great string of black sprinters emerged. In 1956 the black Americans were eclipsed by their white fellow-countryman Bobby Joe Morrow, who took both sprint titles for the first time since Owens; and in 1960, almost out of the blue, and for the first time in Olympic history, both titles went to Europeans, the 100 metres to the German Armin Hary and the 200 metres to Livio Berutti of Italy.

This was not so much an eclipse as a broadening-out. In these two blank championships (partly blank, at least; both high-hurdles titles in these years were won by Lee Calhoun, and the long jump, too, remained in black American hands), evidence was emerging of a greater resilience in black runners than perhaps coaches had been giving them credit for. Inspired in the post-war years by the example of such as Herb McKenley (by birth a Jamaican, who did his training and most of his running in the United States) they had begun to make their mark in the 400 metres. The unfan-

Gold and silver in London: Harrison Dillard (69) beats Barney Ewell (70) in a photo-finish ahead of La Beach (67), McCorquodale (36), Patton (*right*) and McDonald Bailey.

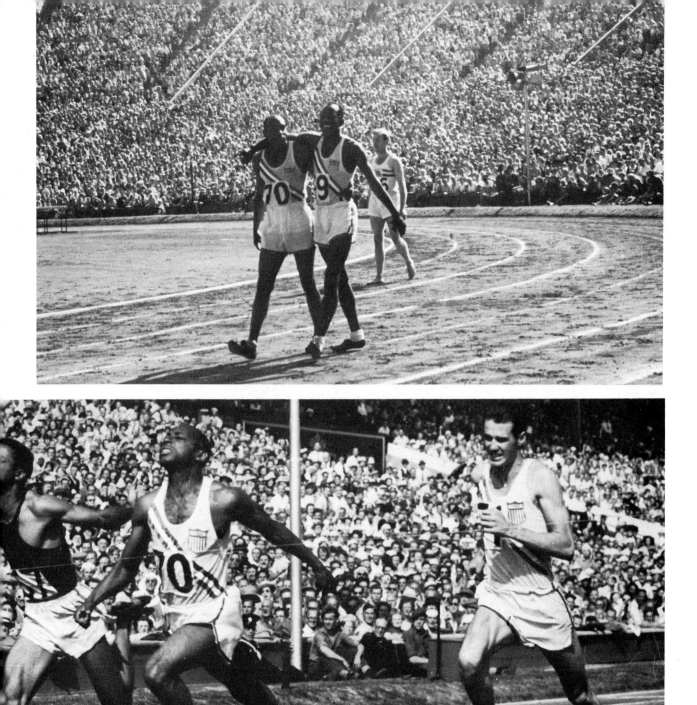

cied Charley Jenkins won the gold medal in Melbourne, and a superbly controlled run, in a world record time, saw Otis Davis home in Rome ahead of the fastest 400 metre field ever assembled.

Then came the 1960s, the post-Kennedy years when the promises had been made but not fulfilled, when black disaffection in the cities and in the South, exacerbated by the conspicuous but unattainable wealth of such a large slice of their society, found its way into the highest reaches of the sport.

In 1964 Black America reasserted its raw power by winning the two sprints with Bob Hayes and Henry Carr, and the high hurdles with Hayes Jones. It was a triumph, but little more than a curtain-raiser to 1968 – the year of the *événements* in France, of the anti-Vietnam riots in the United States.... and the Games of Mexico City.

It was a Games that might never have taken place at all. Mexico was rumbling with civil discontent in the months leading up to the Games, and just ten days before staging the world's greatest festival of companionship and peace the regime used guns and tanks to suppress a student demonstration in the Olympic city itself, killing 260 and injuring 1200 more in the interest of national stability. The Olympic movement, as it is prone to do in such circumstances, kept its head deep in the sand, and the Games went ahead. It is a Games remembered above all for the indelible impression left by the African runners in the longer races. But in terms of the history of the Olympic movement it will be remembered for Black Power, both in its literal sense and its political manifestation.

In terms of explosive performance, black Americans took the gold medals in the 100 metres, the 200 metres, the 400 metres, the long jump, the 110 metres hurdles and both relays. Not only that: in all those individual events this team took two of the three medals (in the 400 metres they made a clean sweep) and in both relays they set new world records.

In the women's athletics at Mexico, too, the U.S.A. won three titles and a silver medal, with every medal winner (including all four members of the 4 × 100 metres relay team) a black American. To cap it all, only two track medals – second in the 1500 metres, third in the 800 metres – went to white Americans.

Black pride was at its height, and if any underprivileged minority had the right to reappraisal from its own nation, this right had been earned by the superb American sprinters of Mexico. Murmurings about some sort of symbolic demonstration had been heard about the Olympic village for days, and it came after the final of the 200 metres. Tommie Smith, the most beautifully balanced,

Sixties supremacy: Bob Hayes (*far left*), Tokyo 100 metres champion; **Lee Evans** (*near left*), **400 metres world-record breaker in Mexico City; Jim Hines** (*right*) **winning the Mexico 100 metres from Jamaica's Lennox Miller and fellow American Charlie Greene (in glasses); Hines takes the baton in lane two** (*above*) **before storming home in the relay ahead of Cuba (in the lead) and France (nearest camera).**

long-striding bend runner since Jesse Owens himself, won by a distance from the brave Peter Norman of Australia and another black American, John Carlos. As Smith and Carlos turned to face the flag for the playing of their national anthem, both bowed their heads and raised a black-gloved hand in a salute of defiance. Smith explained his motives, saying 'If I win I am an American, not a black American; if I did something bad, they would call me a Negro.' The simple force of the demonstration was somewhat soured by the fact that both athletes carried prominently, to the victory podium, a well-known and easily identifiable brand of running shoe. Both runners were sent home as quickly as possible, won something of a martyr's respect among their own people (and, not surprisingly, bitter hostility from a lot of white Americans) and saw their gesture repeated as the brilliant 4 × 400 metre relay squad took their victory medals, each wearing a black beret and each with a clenched fist raised.

Mexico was the high point of black sprinting, and only since the early 1980s have there been signs of a significant revival after some depressing Olympic years in the 1970s, when first Valery Borzov, then some inspired Caribbean sprinters, and finally the Carter boycott of Moscow kept Americans from their traditional spoils in the shorter sprints. Further evidence was to come that black runners were becoming more willing to undertake the rather more specialised training required for the longer, 'harder' sprints (or evidence, perhaps, that conservative coaches had been forced to accept that there was much more to black American running than sheer blind speed). It was epitomised by a tall young student called Edwin Moses who took to the complex and killing 400 metres hurdles with a natural ability that staggered even the Americans. He broke the world record to win the title in Montreal and he was the one absolute certainty for a gold medal who was denied a chance to win by America's refusal to send a team to Moscow. As 1984 began, despite the fact that through his example more black Americans were moving fast up the 400 metres hurdles rankings in his wake, there seemed no better bet

Speed and style: Wilma Rudolph heralded three black American 100 metres victories for women in the 1960s, and won gold medals in the Rome 200 metres and relay for good measure. Tommie Smith (*opposite*) **strode to the 200 metres title in Mexico – and to a momentous demonstration.**

than Ed Moses for a gold medal in Los Angeles.

Black American athletes have made a deep impression on the Olympic Games, and the Olympic movement in common with august international bodies in all spheres of human activity, has from time to time been irked or angered or stung by what it has seen as an affront to its dignity and its status. The black athletes

have pointed out, as Owens did, that skin colour and national origins cannot deny sporting ability its rightful say; and they have demonstrated more than once that the Olympics is the biggest and best-watched stage there is, whether you want to draw attention to a domestic grievance or settle a diplomatic score. But they have also given us Harrison Dillard's hurdling and sprinting, Tommie Smith's bend-running and Lee Evans's incomparable one-lap brilliance, Bob Hayes's naked power and Bob Beamon's unbelievable once-and-for-ever leap. They have given us, too, the half-embarrassed grin of James Cleveland Owens, whom the Germans cheered even when he was beating Germans, and even when they had been told that he was an inferior being.

FANNY BLANKERS-KOEN

THE GREEKS HAD BANNED WOMEN even from watching the ancient Games on pain of death. It does, nevertheless, seem scarcely credible that the high Olympians of the modern era, with Baron de Coubertin always to the fore, should have opposed the entry of women into the athletic arena with such vehemence, vowing, in so many words, that such an occurrence would take place only 'over my dead body'. In fact, it was not far short of that. De Coubertin resigned his presidency of the International Olympic Committee in 1925, so women never ran on an Olympic track under his aegis.

Even when they were allowed in, it took a long time for women's athletics to be accepted as more than a curiosity; the very idea of women in the Games was received sceptically. Their performances were expected to be little more than a weak, slow parody of their menfolk's efforts, and the very idea of women running, jumping and throwing was unnatural and, to some people, positively offensive.

The women's first efforts, at the Amsterdam Games of 1928, didn't do a lot to dispel this view. Very few nations sent a women's team; the sprinting was

Triumphant housewife: Fanny Blankers-Koen (*left*) after her third gold medal in 1948. Triumphant schoolgirl: Babe Didrikson (nearest camera) on the way to her hurdles gold medal in 1932.

respectable, but the high jump and discus produced very tame efforts and the 800 metres, won rather well by Lina Radke of Germany after a long and hard battle with the courageous Japanese Kinue Hitomi, came in for the full weight of male condescension. Several of the finishers appeared at the end to be 'in distress' (it is not fully clear in retrospect quite what that meant, but one would suspect that it involved tired runners collapsing on to the infield after crossing the line, a not unreasonable thing to do after an Olympic middle-distance final); ill-informed physiological and psychological assumptions were immediately used to deduce that women were incapable of running more than a couple of hundred yards without succumbing to a fit of the vapours; and the women's 800 metres was abandoned forthwith.

The climb back has been a long and painful one. Even for Los Angeles 1984 the women's track programme shows the age-old and unjustified cautions against overtiring the weaker sex; no 5000 metres or 10,000 metres for the women – only the somewhat hybrid 3000 metres event which has been included in the Games for the first time as a sop to the long-distance runners, but which in practice produces much the same sort of performances, poses the same sort of tactical problems and, indeed, attracts almost the same top-class fields as the classic 1500 metres event.

This is not to belittle the advance made by women from that inauspicious start in 1928. So fast was their improvement, in fact, that within 20 years their athletic events had become an attraction worthy to stand alongside the men's at any Games – and this even before the entry of the Russians in the 1950s.

Much of this success can be credited to two remarkable – and utterly contrasting – athletes, the first an eighteen-year-old high school girl with an almost frightening intensity of competitive spirit, the other a serene housewife and mother-of-two, shy, retiring and prone to moments of overwhelming self-doubt. Both made Olympic history, both created records that have yet to be equalled, and between them they did more for women's athletics than any amount of well-meaning legislation by well-meaning national Olympic committees could ever have done.

The eighteen-year-old was a thin blonde Texan called Mildred Didrikson, who displayed all the confidence of the professional sportswoman that she was to become. She had already expressed some annoyance at the regulation that restricted her entry to only three of the athletic events (at the 1932 Women's AAU Track and Field Championships she had represented her club at eight events in two-and-a-half hours, and recorded five firsts, a first equal and a fourth place among them); she dealt a further blow to the cause of modest feminine self-deprecation by telling the world's press on the eve of the Games that 'I came out here to beat everybody in sight, and that is exactly what I'm going to do.'

Babe Didrikson was as good as her word. She beat the two German favourites to win the javelin on the first day. She broke the world record (and beat the world record holder) to win the 80 metres hurdles four days later. And on the final day of the Los Angeles Games she took part in a classic battle in the high jump with her American teammate Jean Shiley. Both cleared identical heights and established a new world record; both failed at 1.66m . . . and then by some arcane ruling, dragged out by one of the judges for the first time that day to break the deadlock, Shiley was awarded first place because her conventional 'scissors' style of jump was deemed fair, and Didrikson's 'dive' (a straightforward western roll, in fact) was

deemed illegal. So, absurdly, Babe Didrikson kept her share of the world record but not her share of the gold medal, though by an even more quirky ruling she was given the silver medal rather than being disqualified, despite that she had been using the same 'illegal' jumping style throughout the afternoon. Such is the logic of harrassed officialdom.

Within a few months of her Olympic triumph Babe Didrikson had succumbed to the temptations of the role clearly destined for her from the moment she ran her first race, threw her first baseball or cursed her first official – she turned professional and toured the country as a one-woman circus, running, throwing, playing golf, playing the mouth-organ . . . until she settled on golf

and established herself as the world's best. In 1950 she was elected, by Americans, as the greatest female athlete of the first half of the century, and she remains to this day the only Olympic athlete, man or woman, to have won individual medals for a track event, a jumping event and a throwing event.

Four years later a Dutch girl called Francina Koen, also eighteen years old and with some aptitude, it was rumoured, for the 800 metres (which had, of course, been removed from the Olympic programme), compensated by trying the high jump and rather surprised herself, her father and her coach by coming a very respectable sixth. Two years later a complete change in her coaching programme (her coach Jan Blankers mar-

ried his protegée in 1940) had transformed a high-jumping middle-distance runner into a high-jumping, long-jumping, hurdling sprinter of the highest class, and one can only wonder at the state of the Olympic record books had the War not prevented the 1940 and 1944 Games from taking place.

By the time the London Games came round Fanny Blankers-Koen was thirty, she was in the early months of pregnancy and had therefore been advised to forget the long jump and the high jump (she held the world record for both), and she

The closest of them all: Maureen Gardner was ahead at the first hurdle (*opposite*) **but the Dutch champion was leading (when it mattered) – by inches.**

was written off by Jack Crump, the British athletes' team manager, as 'too old to make the grade' in the Olympic Games.

What prompted Crump to such recklessness is not clear, particularly as Blankers-Koen was also world record holder for the 100 metres and the 80 metres hurdles at the time, but the remark certainly needled the Dutch girl, and it only needed a dismissive 'You're too old, Fanny' from her husband just before the start of a race to add a couple of yards to her pace. In the eight days of the London Olympics she ran 11 races and won them all. She left the field yards in her wake in all three rounds of the 100 metres. She overcame a bad start and the trauma of hitting the fifth barrier to pip Britain's Maureen Gardner at the post to win the 80 metres hurdles. She woke up in tears, overwhelmed by her sudden fame, on the morning of the 200 metres final, then recovered to win it by seven metres or more. And on the last day of the athletics programme, with the Dutch relay team struggling in fourth place, she took the baton on the final leg and tore through the field for her fourth gold

medal of the Games – emulating Jesse Owens's feat in Berlin and setting a standard that no woman has even approached since.

The history of top-class women's athletics has been studded with performers of this kind of all-round excellence, so that any survey of women's Olympic achievement tends to dwell on these rather than on outstanding individual gold medals. How is it, though, that it is women, rather than men, who have been able to produce a whole succession of all-rounders at the highest level?

First of all, it is possible that we are being unfair to the men. At a comparable stage of their athletic development, men's athletics produced an equally talented set of all-rounders who could run their opponents into the ground over short or long distances. Early Olympic Games had many men doing well in several field events each, and even as late as the 1920s a super-athlete like Nurmi was

Right: **Fanny Blankers-Koen's emphatic 200 metres victory.** *Below:* **two champions in retirement – Fanny with the immortal Jesse Owens in 1969.**

Russia's greatest all-rounder: Irina Press, champion hurdler and pentathlete.

able to tackle a 1500 metres, a 5000 metres, a steeplechase and a cross-country in the same week. When a sport is young, and the numbers of athletes in contention far, far smaller than today's, an outstanding performer could expect to perform outstandingly at more than one discipline.

Only with increasing ability, increasing numbers and, most of all, increasing awareness of exactly how training works on the body, has specialisation become the rule. Once the coaching manuals prove that the training programme for the 400 metres is essentially different from the programme for the high hurdles, the athlete who is working for Olympic gold is going to have to make a choice; there is too much talent about to relax and 'have a go' at both.

Much of the credit for this advance must go to the Russians and, subsequently, the East Germans. The Communist decision-makers had been unerring in their calculations: first, that the most immediate impact any regime could make (peacefully, that is) on a world canvas was through sport, and particularly through Olympic success; second, that for years they had stuck to a conscious political decision to make 'sport and culture' an integral part of their countries' way of life, and allocated funds to train professional coaches and instructors to select likely participants and improve standards; and third, that the biggest impression in athletics, and many other parts of the sporting spectrum, could be made in women's events, where the West was falling way below potential. Western countries were still, to a large extent, mollycoddling their women, still believing them incapable of sustained hard training; the Russians, well aware of the heavy physical work that women undertook on the land and the burdens they had shouldered alongside their menfolk in the bitterest of wars, knew better.

Countries in the West have produced, and will continue to produce, the occasional high-class woman athlete to beat the East Europeans, and she will continue to be hailed by a blinkered Western press as having somehow overcome the Communists' 'regimentation' or their 'relentless driving' or their 'chemically manufactured' representatives. But if a national selection policy means regimentation, and country-wide coaching schemes mean relentless driving, then it is high time the Western countries grabbed some of it for the Olympic prospects of their own women. And while drug abuse, sophisticated and unsophisticated, may have had more indiscriminate currency in the East than elsewhere, their coaches know as well as ours that you cannot manufacture champions by shoving pills down their collective throat, and that selection, expert coaching and psychological determination are, and have been since the Russians first entered the Olympic Games in 1952, the only real key to success.

What was surprising when they did arrive was that for all their new-found coaching sophistication they were relying on their all-rounders just like everyone else – Alexandra Chudina, for example, who won the 1952 silver medal in the javelin, another in the long jump and a bronze in the high jump (Chudina was current world record holder in the pentathlon, an event not yet included in the Games; had it been she would undoubtedly have had her just reward of at least one gold medal). She was followed by the redoubtable Irina Press, who won the hurdles in Rome in 1960 and, once the pentathlon took its place in the Games at Tokyo in 1964, walked away with that title as well.

The careers of Britain's two great all-rounders crossed briefly in those Tokyo Games. Mary Rand had gone (as Mary Bignal) to Rome with the ever-inflated expectations of the British press weighing her down unmercifully, and had returned empty-handed from nightmares in the long jump and disappointment in the hurdles. From Tokyo she returned with the biggest haul of medals won by any Briton at a single Games since 1920 – a world record and a gold medal in the long jump, a bronze for her part in the sprint relay and the silver medal behind Irina Press in the pentathlon. Two places behind her, just out of the medals, came Mary Peters, a hefty, jolly Irish

Tokyo gold: Mary Rand's world record long jump (*above*), Ann Packer's world record 800 metres (*top left*)—the first ever Olympic titles for British women athletes.

girl from Belfast. If Mary Rand had been in the light, fast school of pentathletes, Mary Peters was in the power-and-strength school, and while she remained an excellent technical hurdler and the best shot-putter in the United Kingdom, her speed and her jumping were not enough, it seemed, to give her the chance of greater Olympic success. By the Mexico Games, when she was twenty-nine years old, the gloomy predictions were confirmed, and she slipped to ninth place in the pentathlon, hampered by an ankle injury. Then she took a year off, returned to competition for the Commonwealth Games to win both shot and pentathlon and, crucially, changed her high-jump style to the Fosbury flop. Her performance improved by 15 centimetres in little over a year and at Munich, in the closest of competitions, she beat the pentathlon world record, and a world-class field, to win a gold medal at the age of thirty-three.

At Munich, too, another all-rounder was having the week of her life. Heide

Heide Rosendahl, darling of Munich, in the gold-medal 4 × 100 metres relay team (*right*) **and on the way to a silver in the pentathlon.**

Triumphant in Tokyo: Mary Rand, long-jumper supreme *(above)* and top-class pentathlete *(right)*. Ann Packer, 800 metre novice *(below)* rounding the field on the outside and sprinting for the gold medal.

The indestructable Irena: Irena Kirszenstein won gold in Tokyo; as Irena Szewinska she won gold in Mexico City; as a young mother she slipped to bronze in the Munich 200 metres (*left*). As a veteran, converted to the 400 metres, she won gold again at Montreal (*above*).

All-rounder from the West: Heide Rosendahl of West Germany *(right)* – long jump champion, sprint-relay gold medallist and pentathlon runner-up at Munich.

All-rounder from the East: Irina Press of the USSR *(left)* – 80 metre hurdles champion in Rome, pentathlon champion in Tokyo.

Decathlete of the seventies: Bruce Jenner of the United States *(below)*, world record-breaker and winner of the Montreal title.

Decathlete of the eighties: Daley Thompson of Great Britain *(above)*, world record-breaker and winner of the Moscow title.

Not far behind Mary Rand back in 1964 in the Tokyo long jump pit, and still running in the top class long after Heide Rosendahl had retired, was the one woman athlete who might challenge Fanny Blankers-Koen for the title of greatest woman Olympian of all – not so much for her impact on a single Games, but for her versatility and durability over more than a decade of competition. As an eighteen-year-old Irina Kirszenstein won silver medals in the long jump and the 200 metres, not to mention a gold medal in Poland's 4 × 100 metres relay victory. In 1968, as Irina Szewinska, she won the 200 metres and took the 100 metres bronze medal behind the flying Americans Wyomia Tyus and Barbara Ferrell. In 1972, by now a mother, she won the bronze medal in the 200 metres; then, at the age of thirty, she stepped up a distance to the 400 metres and strolled to a gold medal at Montreal in a new world record.

Specialisation by coaches, as we have said, is bound to make the all-rounder an increasingly endangered species. At Moscow in 1980 no woman won more than one individual gold medal in the athletics competitions, something that

Mary Peters, pentathlon victor in Munich, with her newly developed Fosbury flop which established her in an unbeatable lead.

Rosendahl, like Mary Peters, had been disappointed after an injury-hit Mexico Games, but had since become a force not only in the West German sporting arena, but also in the heady world of student and feminist politics. She established herself as darling of the Munich crowd on the first day of the athletics programme by winning West Germany's first gold medal of the Games in the long jump. She failed, by the ridiculously small margin of 10 points, to beat Mary Peters in the pentathlon and finally, all smiles and spectacles, she anchored the West German sprint relay team to victory over the mighty East Germans for a second gold.

had happened only once before since the War, but performances were improving as fast as men's standards had been rising fifty or sixty years earlier. Proof of women's potential as athletes has been provided by the increased number of events open to them at the top level (despite the traditional sluggishness with which they have been sanctioned by the IOC); the first women's Olympic marathon at Los Angeles will be followed with all the intense excitement that followed Kolehmainen's marathon at Antwerp in 1920 or Zatopek's at Helsinki in 1952. By the Olympics at Seoul in 1988 a woman will put her name alongside those of Nurmi and Viren and Yifter as Olympic 10,000 metre champion, and the sophisticated selection

methods and training programmes of the East European nations will ensure that world records keep falling, though by smaller and smaller amounts as the margins for improvement become ever tighter.

The crowds in the stadiums will watch with an appreciation that is no longer patronising, no longer making allowances for feminine shortcomings, no longer hostile to the idea of such a violation of a male preserve. For that we can thank the likes of schoolgirls such as Babe Didrikson and housewives such as Fanny Blankers-Koen, who brought the world's spotlight on to themselves by 'doing the impossible' with such style when women's athletics was still in the cradle.

Three faces of Irina Szewinska: long jumper (silver medal in 1964); sprinter (gold medal ahead of the Australians Boyle and Lamy in 1968) and 400-metre runner (gold medal with imperious ease in 1976).

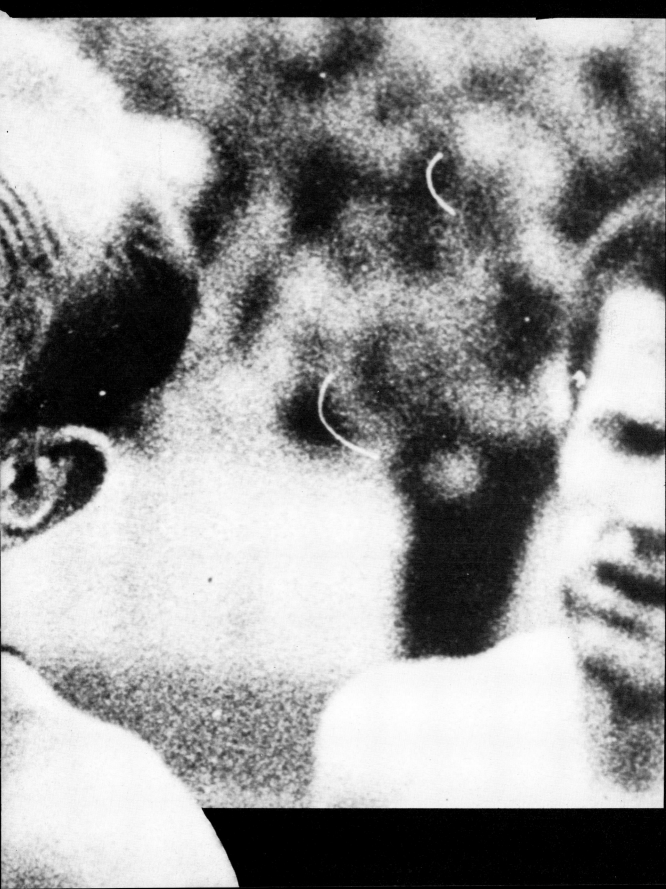

IN THE LATE SUMMER OF 1946, during the first major international championship since the end of the war, a young Czechoslovakian runner, virtually unknown outside his own troubled country, trailed home in fifth place in the European 5000 metres final, the length of the straight behind the winner. All the attention, certainly all Britain's attention, had been on the victor, the slight, bespectacled Sydney Wooderson, cheated so often in the past by injury and by war, now finally winning a major title in a shattering final lap from the Dutchman Willem Slijkhuis. No-one took a lot of notice of Emil Zatopek; fifth place in Europe, even if it is the best run in your career so far, does not rate headlines.

It was a significant moment, though, for world athletics. From that day distance running was to be revolutionised, and a new order would be in command until well into the 1960s. These dozen years or so were to provide an unprecedented, and unrepeated, era in training and achievement, and were to give inspiration to runners throughout the world well after its principals had passed into the anonymity of retirement. It gave immortality and titles galore to two men, and an Olympic gold medal, in its dying phase, to a third. All three, by coincidence, came from what we now call the Soviet bloc: Zatopek of Czechoslovakia, Kuts and Bolotnikov of the USSR – the most devastating long-distance runners since the days of Nurmi.

It is hard, from our standpoint as television viewers of the 1980s, even to appreciate such dominance. A 10,000 metres race has its customary pattern, with which we have been familiar for a decade or two: the strong men try to run the finish out of their inferiors, and the 'kickers' hang on to their heels till, say, the final 300 metres and trust the power of their final sprint against the stamina of the early leaders. Yet from 1948 to 1960, in every major championship (four Olympic, three European) the 10,000 metres was won by a street; in only one of them was there the slightest doubt at the start of the final lap as to who was going to win. Zatopek himself won four of these titles, with winning margins of 48 seconds, 69 seconds (a full lap!), $15\frac{1}{2}$ seconds and 28 seconds; in none of them was there another runner in the final straight when he broke the tape. Vladimir Kuts, his hard, uncompromising

Wembley victory: Zatopek wins the 1948 10,000 metres unchallenged (*above*). Three days later he lined up (203) for the 5000 metres final next to the balding Gaston Reiff.

successor, won his Olympic and European 5000 metres titles by 12.8 seconds and 11 seconds respectively – quite astonishing margins in a race which, before and since, has almost always guaranteed a tight finish. From both men it was running of a class which literally had not been seen before, and each man made an Olympic Games his own.

Zatopek had first realised his own potential in 1941, when he was nineteen, and he had improved steadily but unspectacularly at 800 and 1500 metres until 1945, when the great Swedish middle-distance runner Arne Andersson paid a short visit to Prague. Andersson's physical condition, and the quality of his background work, transformed Zatopek's own training. He added quality to the quantity he had already established, and blended both with the extraordinary determination he had acquired for stretching his own body to the utmost

Zatopek leads in the 5000 metres (*below left*) **and just fails** (*below*) **to catch Reiff with his final sprint. Training in winter snow had given him his tremendous stamina.**

whether in a race or a training session. Even on army sentry duty he might spend an hour running on the spot, knees high, shoulders straight, loading ever more stamina into the training bank. He trained, in those years of his mid-twenties, harder than any athlete had ever trained before. In the winter, when by unwritten law *no-one* trained hard, he put on heavy baseball shoes, or even army boots, and ran through the snow-covered forests – fast quarter- or half-miles with short intervals of jogging between, bounding sometimes in long, looping strides for half a mile at a stretch – observing all the time the effect the work was having on his body.

Coaches today would have channelled the work with far greater economy. They would have tempered the hard workouts with more relaxed sessions; they would have spent hours streamlining Zatopek's tortured, hunched style (a contemporary said he ran like a man who had just been stabbed in the heart); they might even have made him run a little faster. But he had built for himself in these long hours of relentless self-pun-

ishment a capacity for sustained speed – over ten laps or twenty laps – that few runners in the world could match, and a reserve tank at the end of a race to allow him to run flat out for a lap. It was enough ammunition to beat the world.

He took on the best over the grey cinders of Wembley Stadium on the first day of athletics at the 1948 Games. In one of the few warm days of that fortnight he ran the 10,000 metres field into the ground. The Finn Viljo Heino, world record holder and favourite for the title, ran with Zatopek's pace for half the race; then Zatopek surged for half a lap and opened up a gap of ten yards. Heino simply stopped. No-one else got within shouting distance of the Czech, and to the delighted chants of his compatriots in the crowd he won by three-quarters of a lap.

The next day he qualified in the heats of the 5000 metres for a final as strange as it was exciting. Again Zatopek commanded the leading bunch which soon reduced itself to three men – him, Reiff of Belgium, Slijkhuis of Holland. Three laps from the finish Reiff pounced, and opened up an apparently unassailable lead on Slijkhuis, with Zatopek, who appeared to have lost heart or concentration or perhaps just strength, in a hopeless position forty metres from the leader. So they stayed until the start of the final back straight when, with the race as good as over, all hell broke loose as Zatopek began his sprint.

Within seconds he had raced past the tiring Slijkhuis, and began to close on Reiff. As the final bend unfolded, with the whole crowd on their feet roaring, it suddenly began to look as if Reiff could lose. Ahead of Reiff, eighty yards away over the puddles and the squelchy cinders, was the tape; but his effort had come, with great courage, three laps before, and he was nearly spent. And behind him there was this lunatic *sprinting*. As the tape drew nearer, even above the yelling of the crowd he could hear the pattering, splashing danger of Zatopek. He dragged one last effort out of his legs, and the gold medal – Belgium's first ever Olympic track victory – was his. Five yards more, and it could have been a dead heat. Ten yards more and Zatopek would have won.

As it was, it was yet another in a whole succession of breathtaking Olympic 5000 metres finals, and for Zatopek and Gaston Reiff it was only another act in a long-running battle of wits that would reach an even more exciting climax in Helsinki four years later.

By 1952 Zatopek was no longer the raw Czech surprise he had been in 1948. He had broken world records almost at will, he had won the European 10,000 metres with ridiculous ease, and in the 5000 metres, before a disbelieving partisan crowd in Brussels, he had unleashed his famous last-lap sprint and left the local hero Reiff for dead. He was the undisputed master of distance running and yet now, at the age of thirty, he had suffered some unexpected defeats, and he was by no means undisputed favourite for Olympic gold medals – even at 10,000 metres.

Favourite or not, Zatopek's week in Helsinki remains the supreme feat in distance running history, at the Olympic Games or anywhere else. True to repu-tation, if not to current form, he won the 10,000 metres by the usual and tested expedient of systematically running the legs off the opposition – by running too fast for them, by surging whenever he though fit, and by taking a further twenty metres from them in the last lap. He won by a good 100 metres, received his medal, and prepared for the 5000 metres.

He knew that by now, despite his capacity for successive fast laps, he was not really fast enough to break up a 5000 metre field – the German Herbert Schade would be able to lead the field just as quickly as he could; Reiff would be in the field again searching for re-venge; and Zatopek could not be sure that his final weapon, his 400-metre charge after the bell, would be enough to outsprint the young British runners Chris Chataway and Gordon Pirie, who had taken to the distance with such suc-cess. At the bell, Reiff had faded out of contention and Zatopek was positioned perfectly, on the shoulder of Schade who had led virtually from the gun. Zatopek launched himself into the final lap as only he knew how – he kicked, laid back his head, and charged. The crowd roared, and he was away.

Then something happened to Zatopek which, literally, had never happened to him in a major race before. At the start of the back straight in the last lap three men sped past his right shoulder – the young Chataway, Herbert Schade, who by rights should now be struggling in the wake of the Zatopek acceleration, and the French-Algerian Alain Mim-oun. With 300 metres to go he had been striding away from the field; with 250 metres to go he was a mere fourth, out of the medals, his tactics exposed.

He responded almost with despera-tion, but with just the glimmer of a real-isation, as they began to lean into the final bend, that all was not well with the men in front. Chataway, in the lead, was beginning to struggle, Mimoun was closing on Schade, who was in turn inch-ing up to the elbow of the leader. Zato-pek was on them like a lion. With 180

The start of Zatopek's fabulous week in Helsinki: he leads Alain Mimoun and Britain's Gordon Pirie on the way to victory in the 10,000 metres.

The epic 5000 metres: Zatopek makes his final challenge as Chataway leads Schade and Mimoun into the final bend. *Right:* **Chataway falls, Mimoun and Schade chase despairingly, and Zatopek races for the tape.**

metres to go there were four men in a line across the track, and the one on the outside, out in lane three, head rolling, arms thrashing, red vest heaving with the effort, was moving the fastest of all. Chataway, exhausted, tripped on the concrete surround and fell. Mimoun and Schade fought against the numbing fatigue into the straight and towards the tape. Ahead of them, his face a picture of agony mingled with power and pride, ran Zatopek, into the tape and through it – the greatest, most exciting victory of his career.

To say that after that triumph the marathon was a formality is unforgivably to devalue the marathon. Twenty-six miles and 385 yards can never be a formality, and Zatopek had never run that distance in competition in his life.

The perfect climax: Zatopek enters the Helsinki stadium in triumph, well ahead of the marathon field.

But though he might not have known it, his preparation for the long track events had been ideal – the one-hundred-plus miles a week, the fast intervals and the long-striding would today be considered a hard but almost perfect regime for a marathon runner; in 1952 it was almost certainly a better preparation than even Jim Peters – hot favourite for the Olympic title – had undergone.

In the event Zatopek stayed with Peters and with Jansson of Sweden for the early part of the race, and then is supposed to have asked (partly, one would imagine, as a stroke of devastating gamesmanship, and partly out of a genuine desire for information) whether or not 'we ought to be going faster?' Getting no cogent answer from Peters or Jansson, who were understandably quite happy *not* to go any faster, Zatopek left them, accelerated away and arrived at the finish with a little over two-and-a-half minutes to spare, tiring, it is true, but tiring less than the men behind him. The ovation that greeted him as he arrived at the stadium, from a Finnish crowd for whom distance running was meat, drink and mother's milk, bore witness to the magnificence of his triumph. It would need a giant to step into his shoes.

Incredibly the giant appeared, in the guise of a short, stocky, tense, hard-bitten sailor from the Ukraine with a tough imperviousness to pain fired in wartime Russia and honed on a training regime that was so demanding that it almost destroyed *him*, let alone the colleagues with whom he trained. Like Zatopek, Kuts realised early on that he lacked the finishing kick of the true racing athlete, and like Zatopek, whose exploits he admired unreservedly, he strove to build up the maximum sustained pace over a long distance that his body could stand.

He never found for himself the finishing burst that Zatopek was able to command, but in a way he never needed it. Successive quarter-miles at maximum pace in training, with minimum jogging rests in between; six half-miles as fast as he could in a single session, or three top-speed three-quarter miles ... sometimes he had to forego training on the day following his more rigorous sessions, and rarely was he able to train more than five days a week, such was the punishment he submitted himself to.

In 1954, at the European championships in Berne, he did a Zatopek on Zatopek, pounding away at a high cruising speed for lap after lap of the 5000 metres while the Czech champion and Chris Chataway played cat and mouse and waited for the Russian dynamo to come back to them. He didn't; he held on to his relentless pace and left the others to battle for the lower medals.

By the Melbourne Olympics in 1956, with Zatopek now confined almost to guest-appearance status in the marathon, Kuts had taken over the mantle of long-distance king, despite his celebrated defeat a year earlier in the White City thriller by Chataway. It was clear to the world that the only way to beat Kuts now was to stay on his heels, soak up the murderous surges, the half-lap sprints, the strength-sapping fast quarter-miles that the Russian was likely to throw in when they were least expected, and then to race him through the last 400 metres. One person, it seemed, might be able to do it in the Melbourne 10,000 metres – Britain's Gordon Pirie.

And Pirie tried. As if tied to the waistband of Kuts's shorts, mesmerised by the back of Kuts's red vest, Pirie responded to everything – to the sprints, the sudden slowing down, the surges, the sustained bursts of near-suicidal pace – for twenty of the twenty-five laps. Then, the story goes, Kuts slowed down almost to a halt, stepped out into the third lane of the track, and for the first time in the race looked into the face of the automaton who had followed his every footstep for eight long kilometres. And he knew he had won. Pirie, the only man capable of taking on a runner of Kuts's steel, had run himself well-nigh insensible; he had nothing else to give. In the remaining few laps Pirie slipped back, almost uncaring, through the pursuing field and Kuts, desperately tired but by now unbeatable, won with half

Kuts at full stretch – entering the final straight at Melbourne in his punishing 10,000 metres victory.

Kuts's second title – pulling Pirie and Derek Ibbotson to medals as he heads for the 5000 metres gold.

the straight to spare. He and Pirie had run the first half of the race in 14 min 07 sec, roughly the time it had taken for Zatopek to win that pulsating 5000 metres in Helsinki four years before. It was a lethal pace: Kuts had just survived it; Pirie manifestly had not.

Nor could he stay with Kuts later in the week when, unusually, the 5000 metres proved something of an anticlimax after the heroics of the 10,000 metres, and Kuts, with the ease of a Zatopek, simply ran faster than everyone else for twelve-and-a-half laps to beat Pirie by eleven seconds and Britain's Derek Ibbotson by a further four seconds.

Kuts was only twenty-eight, but his health had always been suspect (his heart eventually gave out, and he died in 1975), and it was no real surprise that he lasted only a couple of seasons more at the top. What was surprising was that the man who took his place was a little-regarded Russian runner, only slightly

younger than Kuts himself, who had trailed in 16th and 9th respectively in the two Melbourne races. He had beaten Kuts only once in 1957 when the champion was unfit and out of form, and he had himself not been well enough to contest the European championships in 1958.

But Pyotr Bolotnikov had the full backing, as well as the confidence, of the Russian coaching machine, and he had the application and courage of a Kuts. He came to Rome in 1960 with best times that were undoubtedly very good, but which gave no indication that he was anything like a certainty for a gold medal. Indeed, almost the first thing he did on arrival in Rome was to withdraw from the 5000 metres. For the only time in the post-war era the 5000 metres was scheduled at the start of the week's programme, the 10,000 metres towards the end; with his best chance resting on the longer race Bolotnikov passed up what, with hindsight, must have been a very fair chance of a double gold.

To the spectators it can hardly have seemed a classic. Not until seven kilometres had gone did a breakaway occur, with Bolotnikov well to the fore. Not until two laps from the finish did he make his decisive move. But then it was Zatopek and Kuts all over again, with an injection of pace that was quite unanswerable; Bolotnikov was in a clear lead with 600 metres to go, and he increased it all the way to the bell, into the final bend and to the tape.

Bolotnikov remained in command for one further championship, the European in Belgrade in 1962; but the Zatopek era was at a close, and perhaps he had been lucky to profit from its dying stages. By now coaches and distance runners were learning their lesson – sustained speed was the *sine qua non* of any prospective champion; interval training of a high quality now *had* to be accompanied by long punishing mileage to increase stamina. Speedwork *had* to be introduced to counter any last-lap kick from anyone who had survived the pace.

From now on a fast, level-paced race was not enough. Relentless, lap-after-lap bulldozing could bring world records to such as Ron Clarke, and later to such as David Bedford or Emiel Puttemans or Brendan Foster, but it could rarely win the races that mattered. More 'character', better tactics, subtler coaching, a better-balanced approach, more attention to the build-up to a big race, more analysis – all would bring the achievements of the best distance runners closer to each other, the outcome of a race less predictable, never a foregone conclusion at the bell.

In the five Olympic Games, six European Championships and one World Championship since the end of Bolotnikov's career only one 10,000 metres final and one 5000 metres final have been won by a margin of more than two seconds. This in itself is a tribute to the training revolution precipitated by Zatopek and Kuts. But most of all it is a tribute to their quality as competitors, and a measure of the awesome degree of superiority they achieved over their Olympic contemporaries.

Last in the line: Bolotnikov (559) laps his compatriot Zhukov as he wins the Rome 10,000 metres. *Inset:* **the other Russian, Desyachikov, who finished fourth, basks in the reflected glory.**

HERB ELLIOT

and a brave new world

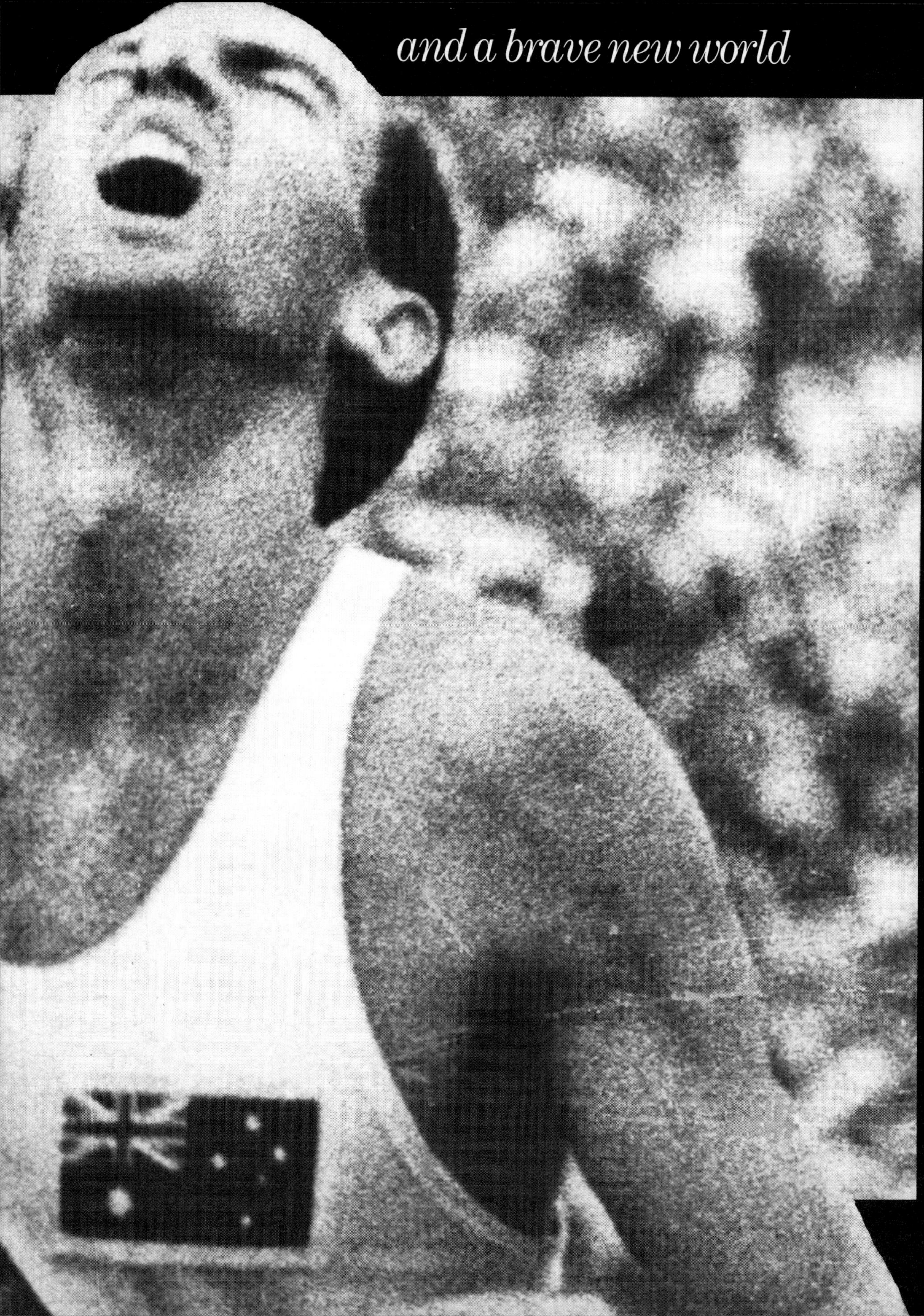

AUSTRALIA HADN'T WON A GOLD MEDAL in a men's track event since 1896; New Zealand had won just one, Jack Lovelock's 1500 metres title in 1936. When the Games were awarded to the southern hemisphere for the first (and, to date, only) time in 1956, they were going to a third world in athletics, with a record of success at Olympic level very little more impressive than that of Africa or the Middle East.

The reasons were not difficult to fathom. All Olympic Games to date had been held at the end of the antipodean winter, quite the worst time of year for an athlete to achieve the peak of a lifetime's training. There were, in those days, no opportunities for Australian or New Zealand runners to join the unofficial European circuit of championships and one-day meetings – such a circuit simply did not exist. And only runners with the highest credentials could arrange an invitation to the college tracks of the United States to train and compete with the American elite.

Even those Australians and New Zealanders who had made their mark had, on the whole, done so away from home. Ted Flack was living and running in London when he won Australia's two track titles in the first Olympic Games. Jack Lovelock had taken a formidable talent with him from New Zealand in 1931, but it was Oxford University and the competition he found in England and Europe that made him a world-beater.

It would be unfair, though, to suggest that Australia and New Zealand were an athletics vacuum. By some curious chance the breakthrough by both countries into home-grown Olympic success came – as it came from the emerging athletic powers in Eastern Europe – from the women. New Zealand's was a minor success, in that it was provided by one woman alone – Yvette Williams, who beat the fancied Russian Chudina in the Helsinki long jump; it is still the only gold medal ever won by a New Zealand woman athlete. Australia, by contrast, had produced out of nowhere a superb stable of female runners, who between 1948 and 1956 captured no fewer than seven gold medals, a silver and five bronzes, chiefly by the efforts of Shirley de la Hunty in the hurdles and Marjorie Jackson and the astonishing Betty Cuthbert in the sprints. This sprint tradition lasted well into the 1970s with Raelene Boyle, but it was at its height at the Melbourne Games where the Australian women compensated the enthusiastic home crowd for the failing of its male competitors, among whom even the great John Landy could oblige with only a bronze medal.

Then, almost by accident, three world-class coaches emerged in the Antipodes. They were actually working many hundreds of miles apart from each other most of the time, but they were also working many thousands of miles from the traditional forcing grounds of Europe and the United States. From that sort of distance Australia and New Zealand had begun to take on the appearance of a coaches' ghetto.

Franz Stampfl, the meticulous Austrian running guru of the early 1950s who included Bannister and Chataway on his list of successes, had moved to Australia as coach to the Victoria AAA. From there he coached Chris Brasher to his steeplechase victory by means of a prodigious correspondence course and a last-minute on-site tuning-up. But primarily he set about building up a squad of runners to rival that of the other great Australian motivator Percy Cerutty, a

Elliott at work: with Percy Cerutty (*opposite*) **and leading Jazy and Rozsavolgyi in the 1500 metres final at Rome.**

legend of a man who held court at Portsea, on Victoria's coast. He had coached John Landy to world fame but not to the heights of competitive running that he might have hoped to attain, and had then discovered Herb Elliott.

In New Zealand Arthur Lydiard was working with a stable of athletes which was, if anything, potentially even more exciting than those burgeoning in Australia. Within eight years of the Melbourne Games Australia was to produce the greatest middle-distance runner of the era, as well as the most prolific record-breaker in distance-running history; and New Zealand was to produce one of the bravest of Olympic long-distance runners, and one of the most successful exponents of middle-distance running in the modern era.

To what extent coaches are the architects of greatness is always a matter for conjecture. If Herb Elliott had not bumped into Cerutty and flogged himself up and down the sand dunes of Portsea, would he still have been a great runner? If Peter Snell had rebelled against the demanding regime of Lydiard, and done more track-work in preference to the long-distance hill running, would he have had the strength (of leg or of character) to progress from 800 metres to 1500 metres?

What is certain is that coaches can inspire, instil confidence, put on the brake when necessary, apply the whip from time to time and act as an invaluable outside observer of progress or problems. A runner and coach in perfect harmony can achieve great things. A coach has never been able to operate aloof, magisterial in isolation, for the simple reason that there are no gold medals for coaches. In modern times it has become increasingly rare to find an athlete who can operate in isolation either, which is why nowadays few great athletes can be studied without mention of their coach and his influence.

It is sad, perhaps, that the Melbourne Games had come one Olympiad too

Elliott alone: racing to a world record at Rome with the field in disarray.
Right: **Halberg the courageous – the last strides in his triumphant bid for the 5000 metres title.**

early for the Antipodean coaches and their promising young protégés. Stampfl, it is true, had his success with Brasher, but Brasher was an Englishman. Cerutty had his Olympic disappointment with Landy, and Lydiard's best hope could do no better than 11th in the 1500 metres final. None of it added up to a fanfare for the triumphs to come.

Stampfl's most likely find had been a young Australian, Mervyn Lincoln, who trailed in last in the 1500 metres at Melbourne, but who was to mature in the next few years into one of the finest of the world's middle-distance runners. Indeed, by 1958 there would have been few people to doubt his claim to being the second best mile and 1500 metre runner in the world. Lincoln's great and lasting misfortune was that he was, at the same time, the second best miler in Australia and the second best miler in the State of Victoria.

This was due to the fact that while Stampfl was urging the best, and that best was exceptional, out of Merv Lincoln, Percy Cerutty was urging even better out of Herb Elliott, exciting him with the very prospect of running, persuading him to put his whole being into his training and into his races. In the 1958-59 athletics season in Europe and Australia Lincoln and the twenty-year-old Elliott met fifteen times over a mile – and Elliott won them all. The list included two major races in Europe: one was at the Commonwealth Games in Cardiff, where Australia took the first three places in front of a British crowd who were not used to seeing their own runners beaten at this distance; the other was in Dublin, where both men beat the Olympic champion Ron Delany. But always it was Elliott first, Lincoln second . . . and so it remained.

Lincoln retired, never having beaten Herb Elliott in a race, and Elliott went to the 1960 Olympics in Rome as clear favourite for the 1500 metres. He had never been beaten in his career at that distance or at a mile, and there seemed no chance of anyone changing that record at Rome. He ran as if to prove his greatness, and his performance in the final was probably more emphatic than any Olympic 1500 metre victory up to that time. From the start of the third lap

he seemed to shift into another gear and, almost gently, he accerated away from the field. The bunch behind him must have known, barely half-way through the race, that they were beaten. They broke up into a straggling procession of tired, forlorn chasers, leaving Elliott to power through the last lap in 55.6 seconds, with Percy Cerutty waving him on frantically from the infield, to break his own world record by nearly half a second and win by a staggering twenty metres from Michel Jazy.

And what, in these momentous days, of New Zealand? For some years Arthur Lydiard had been the force behind a hard, gritty miler called Murray Halberg, remarkable in his early years as a runner for a stiffly held withered arm, the legacy of a boyhood rugby accident, which gave a stuttering, urgent roll to his running style; and for his frequent appearance as a bit-part player in a number of athletic occasions of high drama. At Vancouver in 1954, just a month before his twenty-first birthday, Halberg was on the cast list of 'the Mile of the Century', and finished almost half the straight behind the action as Bannister beat Landy. At the Melbourne Olympics he was a disappointed 11th in Delany's 1500 metres. In 1958 he again watched from a respectful pursuing distance as Elliott crushed Lincoln and Delany in their Dublin classic.

By now though, Halberg and Lydiard had recognised his limitations over the mile, and by 1958 he had tacked his miling experience onto his Lydiard-induced endurance capability to win the Commonwealth three miles title at Cardiff. By Rome he had abandoned the 1500 metres altogether in favour of the 5000 metres and 10,000 metres. In the longer race, run late in the athletics programme, Halberg, like everyone else, was to be decisively beaten by Bolotnikov's surge; but after his performance in the 5000 metres he had every excuse.

In that final there had been no Bolotnikov, no-one to take the early initiative. With three laps of the twelve-and-a-

Snell's first blood: the unexpected 800 metres victory at Rome over Roger Moens (237) and the Jamaican George Kerr.

half-lap final to go, Halberg took off from the leaders in a lap of 61 seconds, a time that would have been perfectly respectable for the second lap of a world-class mile. It was, by all logical argument, suicidal. He might have opened up a twenty-metre gap between himself and his pursuers, but it was a pace no-one could be expected to survive.

Halberg's answer was, for a second consecutive lap, to forget the pain and the fact that when this lap was over there would still be a further agonising 400 metres to go, and to run it as fast as he possibly could. It took him 64 seconds, it hurt like hell, and the gap was slowly being eroded.

Throughout the last lap he was at the limit of his reserves, and it took him an eternity – nearer 70 seconds than 60. In his desperation he looked back again and again at the chasing German Grodotzki and the other pursuers, but by now they were as desperate as he was. As he came, head swimming and muscles screaming, into the last bend he still had ten metres in hand. By the tape, the collapse on to his back and the fight for breath, he was still eight metres clear, and had won a gold medal with the most courageous piece of lone front running that any of the spectators at Rome that day had ever seen.

It was an extraordinary day for Arthur Lydiard's New Zealanders. They had waited twenty-four years since Lovelock's Berlin 1500 metres for a track gold medal. Now they had won two within a couple of hours. The 800 metres was supposed to have been a formality for the world record holder Roger Moens of Belgium, assuming he could hold off the challenge of the Jamaican George Kerr. Moens had eased up in his semi-final to be overtaken by an unheralded young New Zealander, Peter Snell, but everyone agreed that he had the final in his pocket as he took the lead off the final

Snell in command: Assured victory in the Tokyo 800 metres (*below*), triumph in the 1500 metres, unchallenged from final bend (*inset*) to tape.

bend and began his run for home. Then, fatally, he expended time and form looking round to see where the danger might be. It came not from the expected challenge of Kerr, but from Snell, who had steamed up on the inside, and had achieved the full momentum of his final kick before Moens realised his peril. Moens responded, but the initiative had passed to the younger man. Inch by inch Snell drew away to win the gold medal in 1 min 46.3 sec, the third time in three days – heat, semi-final and final – that he had recorded a career best performance.

At that stage in his career Snell had never been considered seriously at any distance beyond 800 metres, but the strength and endurance built into his powerful physique by Lydiard's long-distance sessions and hill running were to pay tremendous dividends by the Tokyo Games. Up to 1962, eight year's after Bannister's breakthrough, no four-minute mile had been run in New Zealand. Snell made his much publicised attempt on a grass track in Wanganui in an international-class field – Bruce Tulloh was there from England, and so was Murray Halberg, back among the bit players again. Not only did Snell break four minutes, he also broke Elliott's world record of 3 min 54.5 sec by a tenth of a second, thus establishing himself as the finest half-mile and mile all-rounder yet seen.

He took this reputation to Tokyo. He won the 800 metres in comfort, after a minor scare when he found himself boxed at the start of the second lap, sprinting away from the field in the last 200 metres and never being seriously challenged. Then he won the 1500 metres with almost absurd ease, turning with a smile of triumph on his face on the final bend – the field way behind him – strained, swaying, without hope of anything but minor medals, much as Elliott's beaten pursuers had entered the final straight four years earlier in Rome.

After Snell there was a lull down under, and a period of Olympic disappointment. Cerutty and Stampfl grew

Surprise in Mexico: Australia's Ralph Doubell beats the Kenyan Kiprugut and Tom Farrell of America to win the 800 metres.

old, and their influence waned. Australia's women still sprinted valiantly, but Australian long-distance running leant so heavily on the record-breaking genius of Ron Clarke that only when he bowed out of Olympic competition with such scant reward was it clear how great was the void he left behind. Her middle-distance running, too, apart from an exceptional victory in the Mexico 800 metres by Ralph Doubell, went into a similar decline, and Australia has since shown signs of a real revival only among her marathon men.

Arthur Lydiard left New Zealand to travel. His reign had been a glorious one, but it had also been dogmatic and dictatorial: his insistence on high-mileage distance-running as a basis for *all* his class runners had produced its champions and, just possibly, burned off an equal number who might have made the grade with more flexible handling. But

his influence had been so great that it was not going to fade away with him, and New Zealanders, as they always will, kept on running.

A thin time in Mexico was partly patched up by an unexpected bronze medal at 1500 metres in Munich by Rod Dixon, and the spirit of the country's runners was underlined by a minor phenomenon who finished sixth in the marathon. Jack Foster had been a moderate club cyclist in Liverpool before emigrating to New Zealand in his mid-thirties and leaving his bike at home. He started running instead, and got rather good at it. He won the New Zealand marathon, and at the age of forty took part in his first Olympic Games at Munich. Almost certainly without knowing

The silver fern again: John Walker leads the 1500 metre field at Montreal with Coghlan (*below*) **and sprints home to win from Van Damme and Wellmann.**

Stalwarts of the seventies: New Zealand's Rod Dixon (*left*) **chases Keino in Munich; Dick Quax** (*right*) **temporarily heads Viren in Montreal.**

it he was providing, with this performance and with his second place to Ian Thompson in the Commonwealth Games marathon two years later, the first tangible signs of the running-and-fitness boom that is now reaching its height.

In the mid-seventies, the pendulum swung back, and, as so often, young men who had been hero-worshipping boys when the great deeds of the 1960s had been the talk of the land, fought to assume their hero's mantle. Brightest of these new stars was John Walker, who had come to prominence in a dramatic 1500 metres Commonwealth Games final in Christchurch by just failing to catch the runaway Filbert Bayi in a stirring finish. Walker matured into *the* great miler of the mid-Seventies, and his storming victory in the 1500 metres at Montreal was a worthy successor to those of Lovelock and Snell.

Walker, after countless dozens of four-minute miles and ever-entertaining 1500 metre spectaculars under his belt, is now past his best. Dick Quax, a great disciple of Lydiard who outran the whole of an impressive 5000 metres field (with the exception of the inevitable Viren) to win a silver medal at Montreal, has graduated to coaching in the United States. Rod Dixon, having been an international force at 1500 metres and 5000 metres for more than ten years, has turned successfully to even longer distances. It is not yet clear where the next challenge is coming from.

But the Olympic tradition is high in both Australia and New Zealand, and while the decision by the latter to join President Carter's boycott of the Moscow Games will inevitably have dampened athletic enthusiasm for a spell, the determination is still there. The green and gold of Australia and the all-black of New Zealand will doubtless be pounding the sand dunes and the mountain tracks of their distant enclave, preparing to mount a fresh challenge to the traditional Olympic strongholds of Europe and America.

WE INHABIT VERY DIFFERENT WORLDS, WE ATHLETES – the track men in one, the throwers and jumpers in another. The struggle for medals is all the same in the end, and the programme on any given day in an Olympic stadium dovetails the two neatly into one another. But if you ignore the fact that we are all wearing the same sort of vests and shorts and tracksuits, you are looking at widely contrasting creatures, divided by different training methods, a different discipline, different preparation and a different psychological approach.

Even where the track and field orbits traditionally overlap, in the sprints and the long jump, the surface similarities only disguise the deep differences. At first glance, perhaps, you might have to look twice to distinguish the two. As the moment for action draws near both sprinter and long jumper can be seen to take off tracksuit top, tracksuit bottom, a second pair of trousers and a sweat-shirt. Both will tuck their gold chain bearing the good luck charm into the top of their vest, both will fiddle with the elastic of their shorts. They will each tie, for the third time, the laces of their running shoes, each take several deep breaths, and each stare, almost unseeing, down the length of their respective tracks: both are willing themselves into the intense concentration demanded from any competitor in an explosive event. At this moment in their ritual they are both in a world of their own: the waiting competitors on the side of the runway do not exist for the long jumper, nor do the other runners for the sprinter.

Before his 100 metres victory at Paris, Harold Abrahams was told by his coach Sam Mussabini: 'Only think of two things, the pistol and the tape. When you hear the one, run like hell until you break the other.' The long jumper, as he waits his turn, has rather more intricate things to think about than that, but both men will move to their marks with the single-minded concentration of a specialist about to perform the job he has come to do.

From that moment their paths diverge. The runner and the jumper become different beings, and for the runner things are rather easier. He comes under the direction of a starter, who dictates his every move until the pistol is fired. Then he is in a race. He may be 'running like hell till he breaks the tape', but he is aware of his opponents; he can regulate his conduct to their performance, he can lengthen or shorten his stride and he can dive for the finish if he needs to. He is *competing*.

No field events specialist has that privilege. He is, from the time his name

Jumper at work (*opposite*): **Yvette Williams on the Dunedin sand dunes. Thrower at ease** (*left*): **the young Al Oerter, soon after his first gold medal.**

is called, as alone as he can possibly be. Everything is in his own hands. It is his decision when he begins his run-up, how fast he begins it, where he plants his feet, whether he pulls up half-way and begins again. He is jumping, essentially, against himself.

Conversely, the actual movements that he makes must adhere rigidly to the pattern he has rehearsed over and over again, session after session, year after year. The sprinter can let the breeze or the challenge from lane five or the roar of the crowd spur him to a quicker pick-up or a longer, more powerful stride. The long-jumper most decidedly must not: once the meticulous rhythm of a thousand practice jumps is allowed to stray, something is bound to go wrong – he will take off short of the board and lose valuable inches, or chop his stride to compensate and lose height and length, or over-stretch and record a no-jump.

Running is natural, whatever techniques are built into it by athlete and coach. A runner's body and mind can adjust to any given situation by speeding up, slowing down, coasting, spurting, minutely changing the angle of the feet to cut off an angle of a bend or avoid the heels of a rival. All field events, bound in by regulations to make each as uniform a test as possible, turn such natural acts as jumping and throwing into unnatural ones which have to be *learned*, and once learned not for an instant in any detail forgotten. Which is why Olympic field competitions are primarily tests of nerve, and why no record holder or pre-contest favourite is ever home and dry until he can prove on the day that he can overcome the tension and behave under pressure just as he behaves on the practice field at home.

On that extraordinary May afternoon in 1935 at Ann Arbor, Michigan, when Jesse Owens broke or equalled six world records within an hour, there was one moment when the pressure might have been expected to get to him. As he stood waiting to start his series at the long jump pit, the man with the microphone focussed all eyes on him by announcing: 'Jesse Owens will now attempt a new long jump world's record.' It takes the nerves of a champion to perform to that

build-up, but Owens had to jump only once that afternoon – he leapt 8.13 metres, the first time anyone had ever gone beyond 8 metres, to set a world record that stood for twenty-five years.

Pressure applied when an athlete is 'fired up' is one thing. Pressure when things are going badly is quite another. At Helsinki in 1952 Yvette Williams was an accomplished long jumper strongly fancied as she left home to take the first ever Olympic medal by a New Zealand woman athlete. She had qualified for the final quite easily that morning, but in doing so she had wrenched a knee ligament on her practice run-up; she wasn't exactly worried about it, but she knew it was there.

Her first effort in the afternoon's final was a no-jump. Her second was a superb leap, high and strong, propelled by the perfect hitch-kick she had honed on the

Opposite: **the first gold medal, in Melbourne.** *Below:* **the third and hardest gold medal, in Tokyo.**

sand dunes of Dunedin over four long years of training. Her jump sailed past the world record mark . . . and received the red flag. It was another no-jump.

With a dodgy knee and nothing on the board to show for two jumps, she had just one more attempt, not merely to record a distance but to join the best six; otherwise she would be out of the competition in the most humiliating way possible. Facing the end of the runway, beyond the pit, was a huge contingent of British, Australian and New Zealand fans, hardly daring to watch. At home the radio station was playing music all night, interspersed with meagre and, to date, thoroughly discouraging news flashes about Yvette's progress in Helsinki. In Dunedin a special edition of the morning paper, with news of a New Zealand triumph, was waiting on the presses just in case New Zealand's prayers could be answered.

And they were. With deliberation she moved back her check marks to make

sure she took off before the tell-tale plasticene strip at the front of the board. Her jump was not a world-beater, but it took her into the top six, and to a further three jumps. With the first of these, her knee warning her at every step that she was not going to have its support much longer, she hit the board fair and square. She soared to within a quarter of an inch of Fanny Blankers-Koen's long-standing world record, took an unassailable lead, and won her gold medal. Nerve, poise and discipline had survived the pressure. The aggression and the pent-up power had been released only at that one instant in which a long jumper can afford to let rip – as her foot hit the board in perfect rhythm – and the instinct born of long practice converted it all into an unbeatable jump.

This battle to combat nerves in field events means that the great world records are rarely set at any championship as important as the Olympic Games (the unforgettable long jump and triple jumps at Mexico City only serve as ex-

ceptions to prove the rule). By contrast, it is the very competitors who can ignore records, and ignore the reputations of any opponent who might have set them, who are more likely to stamp their mark on the competition.

Al Oerter had no time for nerves in 1956 when he first appeared at the Games, as a young man of twenty hardly known outside the United States. He had never thrown anywhere near the veteran Fortune Gordien's world record of 59.28 metres, yet he threw a personal best effort of 56.36m at his first attempt and watched the rest of the field struggle behind him all afternoon. Gordien came close, but never threatened to take the lead ... and the nerves didn't hit Oerter until he climbed up to receive his medal. His knees buckled at the realisation of what he had done, and he nearly fell off the podium.

The nerves affected him rather more four years later in Rome. This time he was reigning champion and favourite, the man to beat, even though another

powerhouse American, Rink Babka, had recently taken charge of the world record. Oerter was so nervous that even after huge throws in practice he almost failed to qualify. And in the final he did not settle down properly until the fifth round, when a throw of 59.18 metres – again his best ever – beat Babka and the rest.

By now there was an aura of invincibility about Oerter, and when the Czech Ludvik Danek beat Oerter's three-month-old world record by a metre-and-a-half just before the Tokyo Games, no-one thought for a moment that this would do any more than spur the double champion to even greater efforts. But for more than a year Oerter had been suffering from the effects of a slipped disc, undergoing cortisone injections and throwing the discus wearing a home-made surgical collar. Then in Tokyo,

The final gold medal, 1968. Oerter (294) paces menacingly outside the cage as Jay Sylvester, world record holder under pressure, prepares to throw.

eight days before the discus final, he slipped over in training and tore cartilages in his lower rib cage. For an athlete whose torso muscles are trained to apply the maximum 'whip' to a twisting, straining frame at the moment of release there could hardly have been a nastier injury.

A masseur was on hand at once with an ice-pack, but the doctors told him that he would not be able to throw for eight weeks, let alone eight days. Oerter demurred. For the first two days he could hardly walk. For the next day or two he was able to run a little, but he didn't go near a discus. On the morning of the qualifying round he was packed in ice and heavily strapped. His first throw nearly doubled him up with pain; the second, equally painful, qualified for the final with a new Olympic record.

Before the final he was strapped again, and given pain-killing injections which didn't work. In competition each throw, 'feeling like someone was trying to tear out my ribs', sailed too low and landed short. Danek established, then consolidated, a useful lead. By the fifth round Oerter was in only fourth place; with his torn muscles shouting for a flat, quick, easy release he deliberately slowed down, went for more pain and more elevation, and heaved a 61-metre throw to take the lead, break Danek's rhythm, and win his third consecutive title.

Pushed into fourth place and out of the medals by that throw was another American, Jay Sylvester, who was soon to establish himself as the world's most powerful discus thrower, raising Danek's world record by more than three metres to a vast 68.40 m by the eve of the Mexico City Games. By this time Oerter had no right to expect a place in the United States team, let alone any realistic chance of another medal. The veteran's back was in no better shape than it had been in the months before Tokyo, and his few decent throws in 1968 had fallen way short of Sylvester's best. But in the arena the very presence of Oerter played havoc with the rest of the field. As he put in a first round effort of some 62 metres, they began visibly to tighten up. As round followed round Oerter prowled about outside the throwing cage, reminding them at every turn

that he was in the lead, that he was the champion and that it was his territory they were presuming to trespass on. Sylvester's style, for all his world record potential, just fell apart, and he finished again without a medal. Oerter, inspired, launched his third attempt 64.78 m, his best ever throw . . . and won.

College boy, champion, invalid and veteran – he had taken four Olympic titles in a row. Three times he had found his lifetime best throw to set the winning mark. And on all four occasions he had taken on and beaten the current world record holder.

Oerter's great displays of nerve and character had also provided the crowds with at least a couple of spectacular contests. All too many Olympic field events finals, though, have been spoiled as spectacles by a first throw or jump, for the first throw is always important, often decisive. The competitor is usually relaxed, if only because there are still two more attempts to follow if he makes a bad mistake; the waiting and the confidence of the opposition have not had a chance to become a worry; and there is always the chance that a well-rehearsed wind-up to a throw, or a familiar stride pattern into a jump, can be fired by all the accumulated aggression built up over the previous hours in Olympic Village, team bus, changing room and warm-up area. If any one of half-a-dozen possible champions achieves a world-class effort at his first attempt, it needs real mettle to counter it. A cool, experienced hand can sit on his bench at a time like this, analyse his own performance, check his footwear and keep his concentration at a high pitch. Any lesser mortal is inclined to freeze.

The Mexico Games, scene of Oerter's ultimate triumph, staged two jumping championships which perfectly illustrated the contrasting reactions to such early pressure. With all the talk of the perils of altitude to distance runners, it was imperfectly appreciated what an advantage the thin air would give the explosive-event specialists – not in a competitive sense, since everyone would receive the same boost, but in terms of personal performance.

Bob Beamon was erratic, temperamental, brilliant or dismal from tourna-

ment to tournament, and was commonly believed to be incapable of withstanding pressure in an Olympic arena. He had qualified for the final only after the worry of recording two no-jumps, but he began the competition with the 'perfect' long jump, raising the world record by more than half a metre, bouncing it, for those who thought in feet and inches, from 27 ft. 4¾ in. to an astonishing 29 ft. 2½ in. Ambitious jumpers had been talking in hushed tones for years about the possibility of a 28-foot leap. Beamon had ignored 28 ft. altogether.

It was a shattering performance. It shattered Beamon himself for months, and it shattered the rest of the field that afternoon. Three men in that final with Beamon were well used to Olympic pressure – Ralph Boston, the champion in Rome and runner-up in Tokyo, Igor Ter-Ovanesyan, the Russian world-record holder and twice before a bronze medallist, and Lynn Davies, seasoned, cool competitor and surprise champion for Britain in the Tokyo rain four years before. All could, all perhaps should, have taken advantage of the altitude and the new tartan surface of the run-up to fight for minor medals and respect-

World records extraordinary: Bob Beamon (*opposite*) **and his unforgettable 8.90 metre leap; Viktor Saneyev** (*below*) **during the historic triple jump tournament in Mexico.**

ability. Each was capable in Mexico City of beating the old world record, if not of catching Beamon. As it was they folded up; not one of them even achieved a personal best. Once the gold medal was jerked out of reach, minds and bodies had collectively refused to take up the unequal struggle.

The same thing could have happened the day before in the triple jump. Here the world record, marginally over 17 metres, had stood for eight years, and though the holder and reigning champion Jozef Schmidt was in the final again, it seemed likely that he would be beaten. In the low-key atmosphere of the qualifying round it became almost a certainty as the Italian Giuseppe Gentile pushed Schmidt's record up to 17.10 m. And in his first-round jump in the final,

The durable Viktor Saneyev at full stretch. Gold in Mexico, Munich and Montreal was followed by silver in Moscow.

Gentile found even more spring and a further 12 centimetres. The field could have crumbled there and then.

On this occasion it didn't. Two rounds later the Russian Viktor Saneyev, whose coach had prepared him to expect a winning distance of around 17 metres, produced a stunning 17.23, to lead Gentile by a single centimetre. Gentile could find no more, but the rest of the field were spurred to even greater efforts. Nelson Prudencio, a Brazilian whom Saneyev had never even heard of, bounded down the runway to hop, step and jump 17.27, to lead by four centimetres. The American Arthur Walker also broke the old world record, but could move no higher than fourth place. And Saneyev prepared for his last jump knowing that he would have to break the world record once again if he was going to win his, and Russia's first, triple-jump title.

He had only one thought in his head – not to foul. He was safe as he hit the board, though not by much, and he bounded through the jarring, punishing sequence of leaps for the last time – to a gigantic 17.39 m.

It had been an extraordinary competition, with the old world record being broken nine times in all, and it produced a champion who was to come closer in achievement to Al Oerter than anyone before or since. Saneyev won the title again in Munich and for a third time in Montreal. In Moscow, at his fourth Games, he nearly emulated Oerter's feat, but not quite. He was close to his compatriot Uudmäe, but the gap remained 11 centimetres at the end, and Saneyev ended his Olympic career with a silver medal. Like Oerter he had performed through pain, against hotter favourites and against advancing age without ever losing his nerve or his form in a tough and complex discipline.

It is unfortunate, but a fact, that even the best field events competitions lack the spectator-appeal they deserve. A whole stadium can roar at an 800 metres, but only a fraction of the crowd can get involved in the tensions of a shot-put contest. And while alert announcers and up-to-date scoreboard displays can hint at drama, only television, which is not always prepared to spend the time, can

dissect and transmit that drama with any real immediacy.

In a long-drawn-out high jump or pole vault competition, where its duration is dictated by mounting achievement rather than by a set number of throws or leaps, the subtleties of the contest can, and often do, lose the attentions of the crowd for hours at a stretch. For the competitors, though, these are the most subtle of contests. They test the nerves, interfering with poise and concentration, in the long waits of the early stages; they continually place doubts in one competitor's mind as they display the confidence of another; and they continually taunt them with the challenge, gradually mounting before their eyes after each successful jump, of a task getting progressively harder.

Perhaps it is for this reason that young girls, particularly, have been able to make their mark in the high jump, even at Olympic level – girls like Babe Didrikson and Dorothy Odam in the 1930s, or the sixteen-year-old Ulrike Meyfarth, urged on and ever upwards by her German compatriots in Munich. They have been able to excel before they have had enough experience and sleepless nights and memories of failure to plague their thoughts and tighten up their reflexes in front of an expectant crowd. And perhaps for the same reason the great performers, having once conquered those nerves, are often able to remain at the top for a long time.

It has always been the mark of a great field events competitor that once the complicated techniques have been mastered and laid as a foundation for success, he or she has had the ability to assess every turn of the contest with coolness and deliberation, and direct the body to maximum effect at the right time.

That is why we remember Bob Beamon for one great jump, but not as a great competitor. That sort of distinction is reserved for the pole vault king of the Fifties, Bob Richards, or the high-leaping Iolanda Balas in the Sixties. And above all, now that standards are even higher and margins for error so much smaller, for such outstanding multiple champions as Viktor Saneyev and Al Oerter.

THE ARRIVAL OF AFRICA AT OLYMPIC GLORY could not have been heralded in a more dramatic, more fitting way. Well into the evening of 10 September 1960 a lithe, mustachioed Ethiopian, whose name was a mystery to almost every one of the applauding Italians lining the Appian Way, glided barefoot towards the Arch of Constantine. He was well ahead of the Moroccan soldier Rhadi ben Abdesselem with whom he had shared the lead for more than half the race. He was fresh, he was still going faster than anyone else in the field, and he was going to win the Rome Marathon.

No-one shouted the name of Abebe Bikila, because no-one really knew who he was, this bodyguard of Haile Selassie, as he reached the last historic landmark of the route, the Obelisk of Axum which, by some special irony, had some twenty years before been plundered from his own homeland by Mussolini. In the cool of the evening he made his final turn, swinging steadily into the final kilometre. He ran strongly down that last straight to the applause of a somewhat subdued crowd, and flung his hands in the air as he crossed the line. He waved away the proffered blanket, submitted himself to the wild, joyous hugs of his Swedish coach Onni Niskanen and, with a certain unhurried gravity, received his gold medal – the first won by a black African in the history of the Games.

The Olympic debut of Africa, where for years both sportsmen and anthropologists had recognised a rich seam of talent, was a long time in coming, chiefly because of the patronising attitude of the big colonial powers – German, Dutch, French, British – towards the native population and its recreational needs, but also because of the lack of any innate desire in most African cultures actually to compete.

African men, many hundreds and thousands of them, spend much of their mobile life running – it is as natural to the Nandi tribe of Kenya as it is to walk; certainly as natural as it is to get on a bus or a bicycle. In hilly country there is little transport, even for the comfortably off; distances are huge by Western standards and even for a Nandi tribesman time does not stand still. So he saves time by running – running to his meetings, running to market, running with messages, running to meet his lover, running because it is just as satisfying as walking but doesn't take so long. Kip Keino ran fifteen miles a day to and from school, and he was no underprivileged exception. It could only be a matter of time in the twentieth century before Africans started running for sport.

Africa's political history ensured that at least a few athletes from the north made their mark in the 'middle ages' of the Olympic movement under the flag of France. Two of them, both Algerians and therefore technically Frenchmen, were outstanding. First Boughèra El Ouafi astonished the world by breaking the Finnish distance domination in Amsterdam in 1928 to win the marathon; and in Melbourne Ali Mimoun O Kacha, better known as Alain Mimoun, crowned a distinguished post-war career by repeating El Ouafi's marathon feat. But Bikila's victory in Rome signified more than that. The new challenge had come from Africa's very heartland, and within eight years black African achievement on the Olympic stage had ensured that the presence of any African in a top-class field would no longer be dismissed without close examination.

In 1964, at Tokyo, Bikila returned, and took back his marathon title by a margin of more than four minutes, allowing himself the frivolity of a few 'bicycle' exercises on his back in the infield and a smiling – he didn't smile much – lap of honour before anyone else appeared in the stadium. His appendix had been removed just five weeks before. By now, though, he was no longer the single standard-bearer of the African surge. A young Kenyan, Wilson Kiprugut, followed Peter Snell home to win a

Ethiopian gold: Abebe Bikila leads Rhadi down the Appian Way in the Rome marathon (*inset*), **and wins the Tokyo race by more than four minutes.**

bronze medal in the 800 metres. And in the last lap of the 10,000 metres a dark Tunisian soldier from the mountainous south of his country, Mohamed Gammoudi, drove past Ron Clarke only to find that, having beaten the world record holder and favourite, he was still not good enough to hold off the unregarded Billy Mills. Pursuing all three of them home in that race was another Ethiopian, a gaunt thirty-two-year-old, Mamo Wolde; and run out of the medals in a slow-run 5000 metres was the twenty-four-year-old Kenyan policeman Kipchoge Keino.

Nobody made a lot of it at the time, but these five Africans had one thing in common. They lived much of the time, and they all trained, at high altitude, where the atmosphere is thinner, forcing the body, over a period, to process the less plentiful oxygen more efficiently.

It was an utter coincidence that in the decade when Africa came out of its athletics shell the International Olympic Committee should, in its wisdom, choose to hold an Olympic Games at altitude for the first time. For that very reason the African running explosion of 1968 has been down-graded, even dismissed as a freak of geographical favouritism, a verdict which is hardly borne out by African performances at sea-level in the years immediately following the Mexico Olympics.

The fact that altitude gave long-distance runners an advantage if their bodies were used to it is not in question. What is less clear is whether the Africans would have swept the board in the longer track events in quite the way that they did if there had not also been a genuine revolution in African running in the years leading up to Mexico. Almost certainly they would not, which suggests that Africa was lucky to get Mexico City at the height of its fresh, precocious new powers ... and the people of Mexico City were indeed lucky to get the Africans.

The impact was undeniable. At every distance from 1500 metres to the marathon, African runners took the gold medal. In the 5000 metres and the 10,000 metres all three medallists were Africans; so were the gold and silver medallists in the steeplechase. Keino,

Four times champion: the young Al Oerter winning the discus in Melbourne (*top left*) **and the veteran Al Oerter repeating himself in Mexico** (*above*).

Three times champion: Viktor Saneyev at Moscow adding a silver to his three triple-jump gold medals.

African arrival: Kipchoge Keino at speed
(*top*) leading from the young Ben Jipcho in his
triumphant 1500 metres at Mexico City;
Kenio at rest (*above*); Keino on new ground
(*right*) winning the Munich steeplechase at
his first attempt at the event.

African advance: John Akii-Bua in full flight
(*top*) and on the roads of Uganda (*above*);
Ben Jipcho on his way to a silver medal
behind Keino in the 1972 steeplechase (*left*).

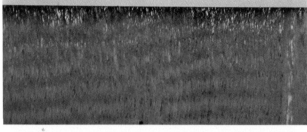

African attitudes: Filbert Bayi of Tanzania (*top left*), miler turned steeplechaser, winning silver in Moscow; Amos Biwott (*above*), ungainly steeplechaser, winning surprise gold at Mexico City.

Mamo Wolde of Ethiopia (*left*), marathon champion four years earlier, winning a courageous bronze at Munich.

in his third Games, and in the 5000 metres gave best only to the remarkable Viren. Following Viren home in the 10,000 metres was a new name from Ethiopia, one Miruts Yifter, whose bronze medal led to comments of regret that he hadn't been discovered earlier, since at his age, it seemed, it was probably too late for him to have another chance. The Kenyans took advantage of various internal breakdowns in American team management – and the consequent absence of an American team – to break a twenty-year run of United States titles in the 4 × 400 metres relay. And Uganda came up with one of the most exciting newcomers of the Games, the scarlet-clad John Akii-Bua, who beat the world record and the Olympic champion simultaneously to win the 400 metres

Frustration and fulfilment: Ethiopia's Mamo Wolde, just beaten into second place in the Mexico 10,000 metres (*left*) **makes up for it** (*below*) **with victory in the marathon.**

Kenyan emergence: the untutored Amos Biwott (*page 124*) **wins the Mexico City steeplechase and Naftali Temu** (*above*) **takes the 10,000 metres**

undoubtedly the track athlete of the Games, won the most emphatic 1500 metres victory in Olympic history in beating the American Jim Ryun. In the 10,000 metres, having joined the decisive breakaway with Temu, Wolde and Gammoudi, he dropped out three laps before the finish when he was caught with stomach cramps. In the 5000 metres a blazing sprint finish saw him lose by a mere fifth of a second to Gammoudi. The Tunisian himself won a gold and a bronze medal. The Kenyan Temu also won a gold and a bronze, and Wolde won a gold in the marathon to add to his 10,000 metres silver.

And everyone waited for them to come down to sea level, to see how good they *really* were. There was no disappointment: Keino remained for another four years the most versatile and talented middle- and long-distance runner in the world; Wolde took over the father-figure role in Ethiopia from Bikila, who had been badly injured in a motor accident; Kenya began to produce runners at shorter distances, with likely-looking contenders at 800 and 400 metres; and the young, fresh-faced Ben Jipcho, who had unselfishly made the pace in Keino's victory over Ryun, began to be spoken of as the master's logical successor.

At Munich there was something of a decline after the heady days of Mexico, but the Africans still made their mark. Gammoudi was still there, strong as ever

The African master: Kipchoge Keino in training (*left*) **and in an all-African battle in the Mexico 5000 metres** (*above*). **The order was unchanged at the finish: Gammoudi, Keino, Temu.**

hurdles with the widest grin imaginable.

Back, too, came Keino. It is a general rule among the greatest and most durable runners that the older and more experienced they get, the longer the events they specialise in. Keino, never the conformist, cut out the 5000 metres and 10,000 metres altogether, had another tilt at the 1500 metres for which he was champion, and took a flier at the 3000 metres steeplechase. He had never tackled the event at any international meeting before, and his hurdling style was as ungainly as his running style between the barriers was faultless. In the final he was up against his compatriot Ben Jipcho, technically a much more accomplished steeplechaser, as well as the extraordinary Amos Biwott, whose unsophisticated attack on the steeplechase at Mexico had come in for nothing but ridicule until he waltzed off with the gold. For a time in the Munich final there was the distinct possibility of a Kenyan clean sweep, but Biwott faded from the attack in the final lap, leaving Keino and Jipcho, with Keino always the stronger, to battle out the first two places. With one Munich gold medal under his belt, Keino must have been immensely confident of a second in the 1500 metres, and with a lap to go he had run the finish out of everybody in the field but one, the Finn Vasala, who astonished the crowds, and possibly even himself, by clinging to Keino's heels, attacking as the final bend unwound, and decisively outkicking the champion.

What African athletics now needed was a period of retrenchment, a year or two for the excitements of Mexico and Munich to sink in, for youngsters of a new generation to respond to their current heroes, and for Africa to consolidate itself in world-class athletics. Such a response from the grassroots depends always on example, and for a while there was example a-plenty, particularly from Africa's Commonwealth Games contenders at Christchurch in 1974. Jipcho established his credentials at last with two gold medals and a bronze, and Kipkurgat and Boit began to assert themselves. Africans from three different nations took the first three places in the 400 metres, and the crowd was thrilled to the core by a gun-to-tape world record in the 1500 metres by Tanzania's first real star, Filbert Bayi. Africa was broadening its base, and all would surely be reinforced by success at Montreal.

What a series of confrontations it would have been. Could Bayi still cope with a maturer John Walker? How was Viren or Brendan Foster going to deal with Yifter? Surely no-one was in the same league as Jipcho in the steeplechase? Could a regenerated John Akii-Bua stand up to a certain young

Edwin Moses in the 400 metres hurdles?

Answer came there none. In response to a New Zealand rugby series played against the outlaw South Africa in the

Steeplechasers all: Keino (*left*) **leaps high at the Munich water jump on his way to victory. Second was his gifted compatriot Ben Jipcho** (*below*)

teeth of Commonwealth opposition, a number of African countries demanded New Zealand's expulsion from the Games. The IOC refused to exclude New Zealand, so twenty-two African nations, at the last possible moment with their athletes trained to a peak and the focus of all eyes in the Olympic Village, pulled out of Montreal.

Never mind, they said, after the Games was over and the disappointment had died down. We'll see them all in Moscow, and we'll see the new Kenyan

Spread of talent: Uganda's John Akii-Bua (*far left*) **receives his 400 metres hurdles gold medal at Munich. Tanzania's Filbert Bayi graduated from 1500 metres to steeplechase.**

wonder-runner Henry Rono, who's beginning to break world records all over the place. A pity about Jipcho, who turned to a professional circuit in desperation. And a pity about Yifter, they said, but he'll probably be in a geriatric ward by Moscow.

Politics and the mysteries of apparent agelessness confounded the prophets yet again. The boycott of Moscow, this time orchestrated by the United States in protest against the host nation's invasion of Afghanistan, was far more significant in terms of medals – and thus the distortion of world athletic accomplishment – than it had been in 1976. But only Kenya among the major African athletics powers stayed away (thereby leaving an eternal question mark over the career of Henry Rono). Bayi almost achieved what Keino had achieved eight years earlier by moving into the unfamiliar territory of the steeplechase and running, rather than steeplechasing, into a wide lead. Rather to the relief of the steeplechasing fraternity the specialist Malinowski pulled back to win with some ease.

Yifter, though, belied age and earlier frustrations, earned himself the admiring nickname 'The Shifter' with his murderous pace suges and his devastating finish, and joined the ranks of Kolehmainen, Zatopek, Kuts and Viren by winning both long-distance track events at the same Games. Indeed, the Ethiopians threatened to emulate the all-conquering Finns of 1936 by sweeping the board in the 10,000 metres, and only a desperate and somewhat unexpected piece of courageous last-lap running by the Finn Maaninka kept the Ethiopian score to first, third and fourth on the final result sheet.

African athletics, whose future seemed to be assured by the late 1960s, has lost a lot of momentum since. Kenya, particularly, should now be looking to a whole new generation, inspired in their youth by Keino, Jipcho and the rest, challenging at every distance over 800 metres. But their absence from two consecutive Olympic Games has, it seems, cast some doubt over the sport's popularity. Certainly the surge of enthusiasm which follows an Olympic triumph cannot so easily be fired by softer victories in African Games, or by the long, willing and good-natured European circuit-bashing by an ageing but ever-popular Mike Boit. Elsewhere there is more depth than there ever was, from Tanzania and Uganda in the South, to Ethiopia in the East (where surely they cannot always come up with a Bikila or a Yifter to order) and to some inspiring challengers from the Arab countries to the north. What Africa needs, black Africa especially, is a repeat, if only in a modest way, of the unrestrained excitement of 1968, when the African sun shone over Mexico City and a whole new dimension was added to the Olympic Games.

The Shifter: Miruts Yifter overcame the threat of Viren to win the 10,000 metres, and his fellow Ethiopians to win the 5000 metres in Moscow.

DALEY THOMPSON

'NINE MICKEY MOUSE EVENTS FOLLOWED BY A SLOW 1500 METRES' is how Steve Ovett is supposed to have described the decathlon in a light-hearted exchange of pleasantries with that event's greatest current exponent Daley Thompson. Whether or not Steve actually said it, or whether it was all a figment of Daley's well publicised, and in many ways justified, paranoia about the public's attitude to the love of his life, is not really clear. But the description certainly sums up the way 'specialist' athletes, and consequently athletics crowds throughout the world, tend to have viewed the decathlon for most of this century.

Even that word 'specialist' seems to denigrate the decathlon, as if somehow a pole-vaulter or a hurdler or a shot-putter takes his own event more seriously than the all-rounder, the jack of all trades and master of none, who has to make do with an artificial mish-mash of physical tests to determine his breadth of strength, skill, speed and talent. It is an attitude which only in the last few years we have been learning – with none-too-gentle prompting by Daley Thompson and his colleagues – to modify.

The concept of the 'super-athlete', one who could outrun, outjump and outthrow any other man, was a fundamental ingredient of the Ancient Greek Olympic Games. It was not, though – possibly for administrative reasons – part of that legacy which Baron de Coubertin and his co-founders of the modern Olympics felt obliged to make part of their new celebrations in the early years. But the Americans had for some time been keen on athletes taking part in 'all-round championships' of various punishing sorts, and they included such a multiple test as a sideshow to the 1904 Games in St Louis.

The Swedes, with characteristic seriousness, took up the task, and after a lot of thought and experiment they devised a series of disciplines fully to test an all-round athlete. They were the very ten tests that make up the decathlon today,

The great Jim Thorpe – master athlete of Stockholm, victim of sanctimonious officialdom.

and the Swedes, as hosts, included the event in the Stockholm Games of 1912, along with a pentathlon for men along similar but less exacting lines.

The record books show that the Swedes took all three medals in Stockholm, and there is the suspicion that if that had been the whole story the rest of

the world might well have quietly forgotten the decathlon and dropped it from the athletics programme altogether. But apart from the odd footnote in small type, the record books omit the name of Jim Thorpe.

Every American sports enthusiast knows the name of Jim Thorpe, as every Englishman knows the name of W. G. Grace. Had the Stockholm Olympics never taken place Jim Thorpe would still remain a legend as a high-class baseball player and a veritable giant in the annals of American football. At the Carlisle School, a minor college in Pennsylvania for full-blooded or half-caste American Indians, Jim Thorpe (a member of the Sac and Fox tribe by birth) was the unstoppable force with which the college football team carved a swathe of victories through some of the most distinguished and powerful sports universities of that era. When the professional game took its early, faltering steps at the time of the First World War, Thorpe was its most feared and most talented exponent; and in 1950 he was far-and-away top of the poll for the United States' Greatest Sportsman of the Half-Century.

At the Stockholm Games, after very little training, Thorpe won the pentathlon by a wide margin, and then the decathlon by a staggering 700 points (representing a superiority over the next man of rather more than ten per cent). In five of the ten disciplines he was the best in the field; in only one, the long jump, was he as low as fourth. And the totals he amassed overshadowed all competitors in all decathlon competitions for the next fifteen years. The unquestioning sanctimoniousness which allowed the International Olympic Committee, at the drop of a newspaper story, to strip Thorpe of his medals because he had once been paid peanuts for playing baseball in the college vacation reflects no credit at all on the movement, no less because it took them 70 years – well after Thorpe himself had died in poverty – to change their minds and reinstate him and his performances to their rightful place in the records. But Thorpe's feats

Bob Mathias: schoolboy revelation (*left*) **in London in 1948; mature superdecathlete** (*right*) **in Helsinki four years later.**

of 1912 (they would have kept him at the top of the British decathlon listings as late as 1962) fired America with the excitement of the event's possibilities, and assured it an Olympic future.

For the next forty or fifty years the Olympic decathlon settled down as a confrontation between the 'American' style of decathlete and the 'Scandinavian' style. The 'American' would tend to be a specialist athlete who would pile up points in his special skill – the discus or the 400 metres, for example –

score strongly in those events which responded well to his specialist training, and survive in the others. Most conspicuous of these was Harold Osborn. In 1924 he won the individual gold medal in the high jump as well as winning the decathlon (an individual/combined double which has never been equalled); and there were a number of great names in the following years who relied on similar top-heavy series of performances to get them to the top. Jim Bausch, the American who won in Los Angeles in

1932, was a huge heavyweight whose shot and discus points made up for his lack of speed; and Glenn Morris, who was to seek his fortune as an actor in Hollywood after winning the decathlon in Berlin, forsook the hurdles for the all-round competition only in the year of the Games.

The 'Scandinavian' exponents, by contrast, tackled the event at its fundamentals, arguing the need for a high mean performance at all ten disciplines. They would work consciously on their weaker events rather than their strong ones, fighting all the time to improve the average rather than blasting ahead in some areas and scraping through in others. Most successful among the 'Scandinavian' decathletes were two Finns, Paavo Yrjola, who won the title in Amsterdam, and Aki Jarvinen, who was second to Yrjola in 1928 and again to Bausch in 1932. (One has a lot of sympathy for Jarvinen. Decathlon scoring tables have to be adjusted from time to time in line with the uneven improvement in standards. Under the current tables, Jarvinen would have won both the gold medals.)

The decathlon, though, was still a

Laying the foundations: Bruce Jenner's 100 metres, high jump and long jump on the first day in Montreal.

long way from capturing the imagination of the public. The subtleties of style and method were difficult enough to appreciate even for spectators fully versed in points tables and the fluctuations of competition. In the tight schedule of an Olympics athletics programme the decathlon tended to be pushed to one side, unexplained in the days before the electric scoreboard, and often unremarked.

At London in 1948, the event degenerated almost into farce. It rained for

Reaping the reward: Jenner's javelin, and his finish in the 1500 metres, which assured him of the gold medal and a new world record.

most of both days, and far too little time had been allocated for an unexpectedly large entry. The programme overran by hours, and as the competition drew to an end on the second day the javelin had to be lit by torches and the 1500 metres runners plodded round a near-deserted Wembley in darkness.

The one thing that Wembley did produce was Bob Mathias, a 17-year-old American schoolboy who won the title at his first attempt and emerged over the next few years as the greatest talent that the event had unearthed to date. Mathias was an excellent discus-thrower and shot-putter in the 'American' style, but by 1952 he had emerged as a genuine 'Scandinavian' all-rounder, adding skill in pole vault and javelin to his great talents in the strength events. At Helsinki he was in a league of his own. He not only broke his own world record by 400 points; he won the competition with a margin of 900 points. He retired soon afterwards at the age of twenty-two, just the time of life when any top-class decathlete would nowadays by expecting to move into top gear.

The decathlon in the fifties and sixties was an event waiting for television to come and claim it. There was plenty of material: the 1960 Games witnessed a tremendous battle for the gold medal between two students from UCLA – Rafer Johnson, a powerful black athlete who had won the silver medal at Melbourne, and C. K. Yang in the colours of Formosa, a compact, wiry Chinese. They led the field throughout the competition, and that lead changed hands a number of times. Yang managed to 'beat' Johnson in seven of the ten disciplines, but he came to the final event, the 1500 metres, needing to beat Johnson home by some 60 metres to take the gold medal. Johnson clung on, kept Yang's margin of victory down to a mere six metres, and won the competition by a paltry 58 points.

It was heroic stuff, but it still needed hours of analysis by commentators and journalists to be able to tell the public so. The larger-than-life Bill Toomey

splendidly took the gold medal in the rare air of Mexico City, won American plaudits, and retired. The breaking of the long American stranglehold, once by a German, once by the brilliant Russian Avilov, evoked a certain widening of interest, and then more indifference.

Then, at last, came a breakthrough for the event. Bruce Jenner, an attractive, extrovert American from the East, believed deeply in the essential excitement of the decathlon as a single, unified event. He trained to that end and he worked at it as perhaps no American had worked at the decathlon before. He reached his peak as the Olympic Games returned to North America (and thus to peak-time live viewing by Americans) and he willed the spectators at Montreal to sit up and take note of his deeds, and those of his opponents, rather than slump back mystified and wait for the next heat of the steeplechase.

Jenner's personality forced Americans to accept him as an authentic hero, as valid a gold medallist as Ed Moses in the hurdles. American athletes had been having a gloomy time on the track, eclipsed in the sprints by West Indians, in the middle distances by a Cuban and a New Zealander and in the long distances by Lasse Viren, so Jenner's flamboyant world record had given their

supporters something positive to cheer. But Jenner retired after the Games, leaving a long line of American success in the decathlon without any apparent heir, at just the time when the event might have taken off and flourished in the glow of his victory.

The challenge came instead from West Germany (followed, as so often, by East Germany) and by a lone, but not exactly quiet, British voice – the unlikely figure of Daley Thompson who had striven among the also-rans behind Jenner at Montreal.

Within a couple of years Daley had assumed Bruce Jenner's role as master of the decathlon and, equally as important, as crowd-pleaser, ring-master and public relations officer for the event. The decathlon, always difficult to watch live, was tailor-made for television's 'edited highlights syndrome', capable of being dramatised as event followed event and larger-than-life shot-putter was followed by larger-than-life high-jumper. The public might not want to sit through an epic, but they were willing to be fed a skilfully edited epic in two acts.

Also-ran behind Jenner at Montreal ... and a powerful force in the decathlon ever since: the determined Daley Thompson.

Two days in the career of a top-class decathlete: Daley Thompson at work on the first day's disciplines, starting with the 100 metres sprint, followed by the long jump (one of his strongest events) and the shot-put.

Daley was the natural lead, whether at a Commonwealth, a European, a World or an Olympic championship, making each element of the decathlon a drama in itself. What had been an awkward exercise for marshals and timekeepers, a series of sub-standard side-shows to be fitted in around more important heats and finals, became at best a slowly unfolding dramatic confrontation, to be accorded the full attentions of the public address system and electronic scoreboard. By now it was accepted that a well-informed audience could become fascinated and even, given the right ingredients, excited.

It would not have worked if the new exponents had not been superb athletes – Kachanov of Russia, Kratschmer and Hingsen of West Germany, and Thompson himself. Daley was somehow the personification of the decathlon's advance, a man who had dedicated his life,

for the foreseeable future at least, to nothing more or less than getting better and better at the decathlon. The improvement of standards has been astonishing, even on the high standards set by Jim Thorpe in 1912. Thorpe's victory was won at an Olympic Games which, from any standpoint, set new levels of excellence in track and field – Stockholm was truly the first 'quality' Games of the modern era. Thorpe's marks in his ten disciplines were formidable, and he was good enough to take fourth place in the individual high jump competition and come seventh in the long jump. Yet if the ten performances that made up Daley Thompson's gold medal score in Moscow were transformed to the individual events at those Stockholm Games, he would have *won* the 100 metres, the long jump, the high jump, the 400 metres, the 110 metres hurdles, the pole vault and the javelin;

he would have got bronze medals in the shot and the discus; and only in the 1500 metres, the culminating torture of the decathletes, who simply are not built for middle-distance running, would he still have lagged far behind the field. Even as recently as the London Games of 1948, Daley's performances would have won him three gold medals and a bronze, and seen him into three other finals.

Yet there are still athletes – runners, jumpers and throwers – who see the decathlete as a man flogging his body six hours a day, seven days a week, in order to do ten different things moderately well. Only with Daley shouting at us have we begun to appreciate that in fact the decathlete is a man flogging his body six hours a day in order to do one thing extremely well. The decathlon is a single event, not ten, and its implications for the athlete are therefore extremely complex. A man who wants to put the shot

Day One ends with the high jump and
the unwelcome effort of the 400 metres;
the night can be spent worrying about
the complex technicalities of Day Two,
which begins (and, for the clumsy, can
end painfully) with the 110 metres
hurdles.

The second morning ends with the discus; the pole vault, which often takes up most of the afternoon, can make or break a decathlete's overall performance. More than one Olympic competitor has suffered the humiliation of failing to record any height at all – thus scoring a disastrous zero.

a long way needs bulk and enormous shoulders; the man who wants to pole-vault is happy with the big shoulders, but would prefer a lighter frame; the whipping leg-action of the hurdler is at odds with the power-base hips of the discus-thrower; the explosive power of the long jumper at odds with the light, floating ease the 1500 metres demands. Every event complements another in some way, opposes it in others. And every phase of the decathletes' training has to take this into account.

They have, perhaps for that very reason, become a race apart. The proportion of their training to competition is very high indeed, not only because of the amount of work their bodies have to be prepared to do, but because the events themselves are so rare. A decathlon's requirement in terms of time, equipment and officials is vast, its pulling power over live audiences is small, and it simply cannot be fitted cosily into a lucrative evening spectacular at Crystal Palace or Bislett. The competitors themselves become an introspective group. In a normal field event it is just possible for an athlete to cut himself off mentally from all the opposition and concentrate 100 per cent on his own performance. The decathlete cannot. He has to live with his opponents for two long days, running with them, jumping and throwing against them at different times, always in a different order. As the competition progresses they tend almost to build a barrier between competitors on one side and officials and spectators on the other.

Yet out of that enforced camaraderie the winner must still steel himself to ten superlative performances so as to out-do his colleagues more often than they out-do him. It is no wonder that many decathletes find the psychological strain of the two days every bit as taxing as the physical.

The decathlon must inevitably retain something of its mystique and stay at arm's length from the more popular individual events; it can never possibly have the same immediacy as a javelin contest or a 400 metres. On the other hand, television has begun to discover its potential, and the decathlon is quite as attractive as those junk sports in the 'Superstars' mould that have proved such popular viewing. With Daley Thompson and characters of his calibre to the fore, and given the added impulse of a new star performer emerging from South America, perhaps, or Africa, there seems no reason why the decathlon's much enhanced Olympic status shouldn't go on improving.

The final lap: last but one comes the javelin; last of all the dreaded, draining 1500 metres. For Daley Thompson at Moscow (as so often before and since) victory was virtually assured before the 1500 metres began - the vanquished arrived at the finish first, to be joined at his leisure by their slow-finishing conqueror. Another gold medal for Daley.

RON CLARKE

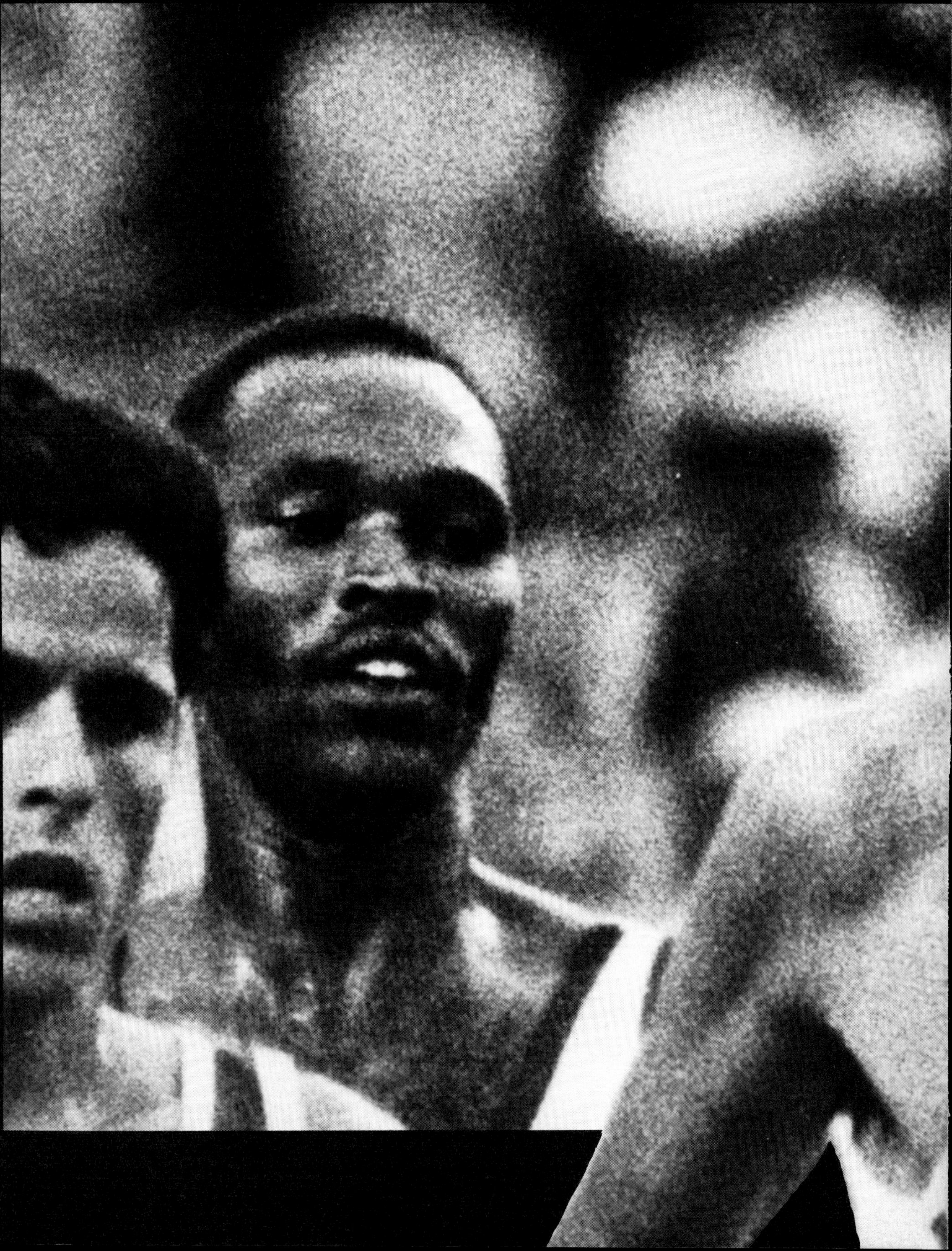

and the 'nearly men'

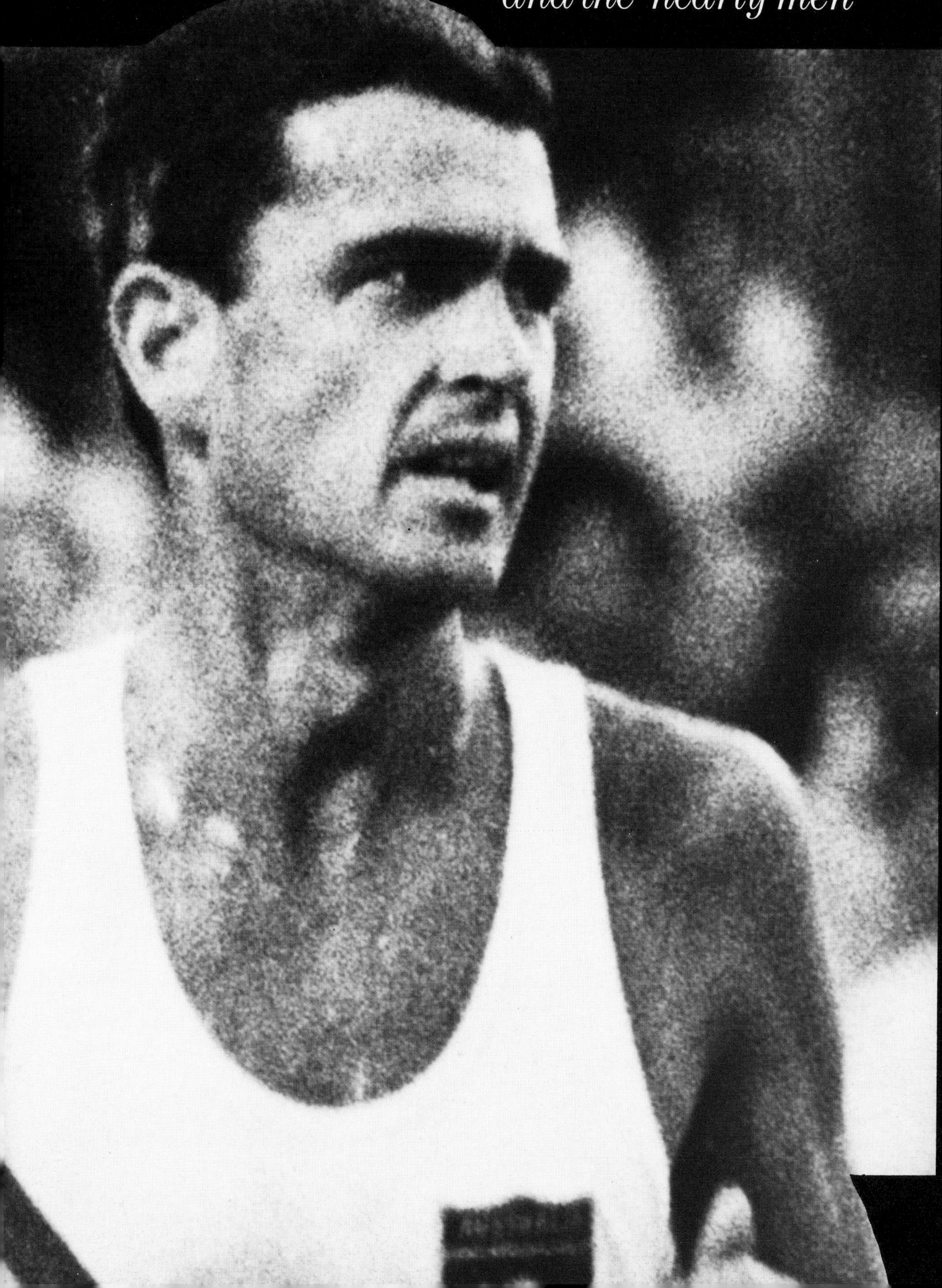

TWO PICTURES STAND OUT IN THE MEMORY. One, from an old news photograph (*see page 156*), is the face of Roger Moens, world record holder at 800 metres, making his desperate last-stride lunge for the tape in the Rome final. From the strained neck muscles to the half-closed eyes there is pain, determination and despair. For a yard to his left, closer to the tape and now certain to get there first, is the young Peter Snell, lunging even more desperately, it seems, neck even more strained, mouth even wider open, eyes screwed almost shut with the effort – but, without doubt, winning. Moens, a veteran compared with his young conqueror, after years of striving, of training long hours, of punishing his athlete's body to make himself the fastest 800 metres runner in the world, is this instant about to become an Olympic silver medallist; by the look on his face he might just as well have been consigned to eternal damnation.

The other image is from the television screen, also from the end of an Olympic final – the 1500 metres at Munich twelve years later. The unexpected winner Pekka Vasala runs through the tape, understandably elated; in second place comes the great Kip Keino, already twice an Olympic gold medallist, out-manoeuvred and outkicked on this oc-casion, rueful, disappointed, but hardly shattered . . . it is not the end of his world by any means. Behind them both, storm-ing into third place, comes the little-con-sidered, almost unknown New Zealan-der Rod Dixon. In each of the three rounds of the 1500 metres competition he has improved on his career best time. He waves to the crowd, he waves to the electric scoreboard he is barely re-strained, it seems, from doing a lap of honour. He has just won an Olympic bronze medal, and he is the happiest man in the world.

In the Olympic Games there are many more losers than winners, more disap-pointments than triumphs. The de Coubertin maxim that the most impor-tant thing is not to win but to take part is admirable and almost universally true – but that does not stop a great many people being very upset at not winning, and does not alter the fact that only a very few people can crown all their am-bition and hard work with a gold medal. Without losers of the highest class we could never set such a high store by the winners; yet the great losers, if they could ever forgive us for describing them as such, are consigned far too readily to the shadows, and the winners,

Hero, but not champion: Jean Bouin, pride of all France, beaten into second place by Hannes Kolehmainen in the historic Stockholm 5000 metres final.

perhaps, granted far too great a helping of glory.

Nathaniel Cartmell, Hans Grodotzki, Ivo van Damme and Raelene Boyle all ran in Olympic finals without ever winning a gold medal – but they share that distinction with hundreds of other top-rank athletes. What actually sets these four runners apart from all others is that, without ever winning a gold medal in their careers, they each won two silver medals at the same Games. Cartmell lost both sprints to his compatriot Archie Hahn in 1904; Grodotzki chased Halberg home in the 5000 metres at Rome, and Bolotnikov in the 10,000 metres; van Damme was beaten by Juantorena in the 800 metres and John Walker in the 1500 metres at Montreal; Rae Boyle lost to the great East German Renate Stecher in both sprints at Munich. Supreme performers all, Olympians of the highest calibre, yet, because of the absurdly cut-and-dried way we look at such things, none of them is much more than a footnote in Olympic history.

None of these four, strangely enough, was really expected to get a gold medal, and of the four only Raelene Boyle ever looked like winning against, in all cases, better runners. Perhaps they remained satisfied, even delighted, with their silver medals, as they had every right to do ... and yet, perhaps not.

How can we read the mind, from back in the Games' misty past, of the man who came off second best in the first head-to-head contest of genuine quality that the Games had seen? The name of Hannes Kolehmainen is held in awe in Finland and throughout the world as father of his country's athletic traditions, and his double 5000 metres and 10,000 metres triumph at Stockholm (followed by his marathon victory in 1920) set him among the all-time Olympic greats. But what of the man whom he beat in the 5000 metres, Jean Bouin of France? Bouin was world record holder at 10,000 metres, but he decided to concentrate on the shorter race and he fought a fast, uncompromising duel with Kolehmainen from start to finish, several times spurting away in an attempt to break the Finn. In the penultimate lap Kolehmainen in turn surged away, only to be overtaken again by the Frenchman

on the last lap. On the last bend Bouin held a four-metre lead; with sixty metres to go the gap had been halved. Down the straight they battled, side by side, for the tape, which Kolehmainen reached a tenth of a second in front. They had both broken the old world record by almost half a minute, and Bouin had established himself as – and in many eyes still remains – France's greatest runner. Yet when he died, a volunteer in the trenches of the First World War, he was the holder of a single Olympic silver medal – a glorious silver medal, it is true, but not a gold medal.

Glorious, too, in their way, were Dorothy Tyler's two high jump silver medals. In 1936, as the sixteen-year-old Dorothy Odam, she cleared the same height as the winner but was relegated to second place by the regulations then in force (today's count-back rules would have given her the gold). Twelve years later, as a mother of two children, one of them only eight months old, she again cleared the same height as the winner,

and was again placed second under the technicalities. She tried, great Olympian that she was, again in 1952 and 1956, coming seventh (with a thigh strain) and 12th (at the age of thirty-six). Was the 'taking part' as satisfying as the 'winning' would have been?

Some of the greatest names, of course, never won medals at all. Olympic competition is cruel, even to the best runners. Stage fright is not confined to the stage, preparation has not always been perfectly gauged, the physical and the psychological have not always come together in unison at the critical time. And other obstacles, dare we say more important, can prove crucial.

The Melbourne Games of 1956, for example, were going to be Hungary's Games. By one of those flukes of time and place and human endeavour, the country that had emerged in the early fifties as the most exciting football power on earth had at the same time, under the coaching of Mihaly Igloi, developed a stable of fine middle- and long-distance

False hopes: Jim Ryun (USA) leads Kip Keino home in the semi-final of the Mexico City 1500 metres (*above*). In the final, the positions were to be decisively reversed.

False hopes: Ron Clarke of Australia leads out the field in the Mexico City 5000 metres final (*left*). The altitude and Mohamed Gammoudi (781) were to prove too much for him.

The complete middle-distance runner: Peter Snell at speed (*left*) and triumphant at Rome (*above*) flanked on the 800 metres victory podium by Roger Moens of Belgium (2nd) and George Kerr of the West Indies (3rd).

The silver fern returns: John Walker wins the Montreal 1500 metres from Ivo van Damme (Belgium) and Paul Wellman (West Germany).

The unvanquished: Herb Elliott, 1500 metre champion at Rome, never beaten throughout his career at 1500 metres or the mile.

Defeat and victory: Steve Ovett drives for
home *(above)* in the Moscow 800 metres,
with Coe in vain pursuit. Coe waits to pounce
on the final bend of the 1500 metres *(right)* to
leave Jurgen Straub (338) and Ovett in his
wake.

The face of defeat (*page 156*): **the despair of Roger Moens as the young Peter Snell steals the gold from under his nose. The unfulfilled: eight years after young Ron Clarke had lit the Olympic flame at Melbourne, he led the Tokyo 10,000 metres field into the final lap only to be passed by Billy Mills (722) and Mohamed Gammoudi before the finish.**

runners. In the record books and the European races of those years, among the Zatopeks and Kutses and Mimouns and Chataways, came the ever-improving, ever-increasing interjections of Tabori, Rozsavolgyi, Iharos.

In the eighteen months preceding Melbourne all three of these runners had broken the world 1500 metres record, and Iharos, at one time or another, also led the world at two miles, three miles, 5000 metres, six miles and 10,000 metres. Medals at Melbourne, it seemed, were theirs for the taking – until the fighting broke out in Budapest, shook every Hungarian to the core, and relegated the remote Olympic Games to a sad irrelevance.

The team was decimated. The great Iharos did not even make the trip. Tabori was well below his best form, and could not manage a medal at either 1500 metres or 5000 metres. Rozsavolgyi did not even survive the 1500 metres heats. Minor Hungarians won minor medals in the 10,000 metres and the steeplechase, but once again time and fortune and the

impatient four-year demands of the Games had conspired between them to create ordinary, vulnerable runners out of champions.

Failure, as Rod Dixon showed at Munich, is a matter of degree. Failure in some eyes is undreamed-of success in others, just as a highly creditable rating on the world scale of excellence can come as the most profound disappointment. For the most difficult reverse for an athlete is to lose the gold medal he or she knows is within grasp, to be beaten favourite, to watch – even to be part of – a victory ceremony at which, everything tells him, *he* should be standing on the highest step of the podium.

It was just that kind of emptiness that I felt that Saturday in Moscow after I had failed to do what for that whole year I had believed implicitly that I was going to do – win the 800 metres gold medal.

To anyone who has started out on a long campaign believing that the gold medal was destined for him, the feeling when, all of a sudden, the medal has gone somewhere else is quite indescribable.

A lot of play was made over the fact that I had lost the final to Steve Ovett, and that this was the real disappointment. It was absolutely nowhere near the truth; Steve did not enter into it at all, and it would not have mattered to me who had won. That gold medal was something I had envisaged, dreamed about, physically worked for, almost assumed was mine; that evening there was just a complete void.

And one thing is certain. The fact that I had won the silver medal – something I'm sure thousands of other athletes would have given their right arm for – was absolutely no consolation at all. It's utter idiocy to say 'first is first, second is

The impossible task: high altitude and the altitude-trained Africans beat Clarke twice in Mexico City. After the 10,000 metres he collapsed insensible.

nowhere', but that evening it would have expressed my feelings exactly.

Jim Ryun would have understood it, too. Ryun was the best middle-distance runner that the United States had ever produced. He had also been their most precocious, and in 1964, when he was only seventeen, he had won selection to the Tokyo Olympics only to suffer his first big-occasion reverse, a cold, which hampered his running and prevented him reaching the final.

Within two years, though, he was the fastest in the world. In 1967 he decisively beat Kip Keino in a sensationally fast 1500 metres which knocked a

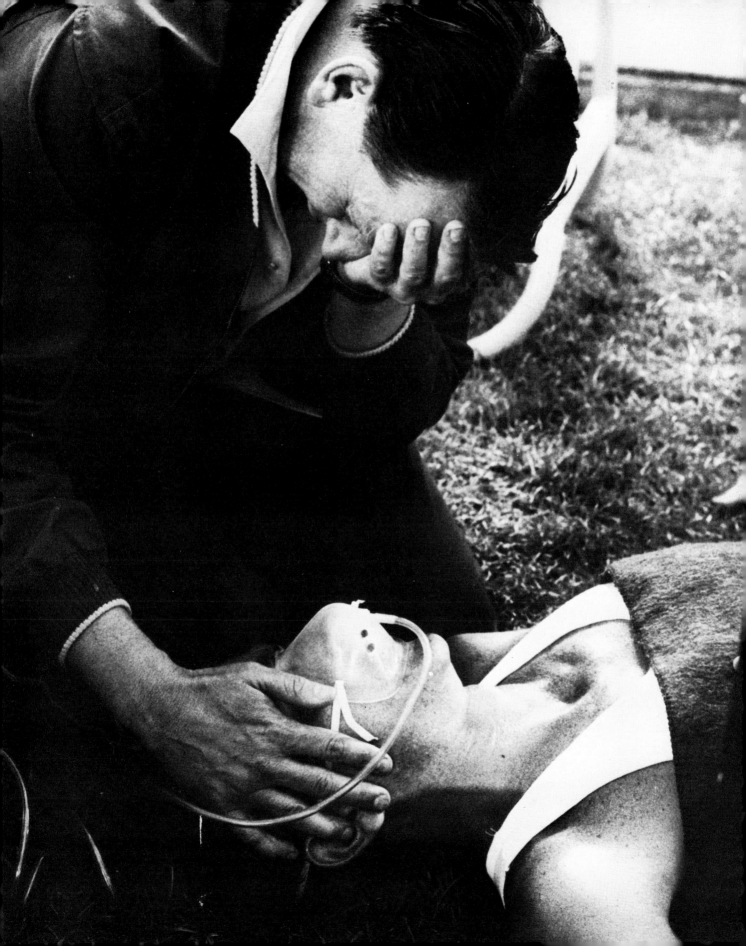

full two-and-a-half seconds off Herb Elliott's world record. He was world mile record holder, too, and by the time he came to the heights of Mexico City he had been training systematically at altitude to combat the effects of the thin air. Perhaps, in the event, it was the altitude that beat him, but his plan (to run three steady 60-second laps and follow them with an all-out 300 metres sprint to the finish) reckoned without Keino. The African was pulled along by his compatriot Ben Jipcho to a murderous 56-second first lap, followed by a second in an equally sapping 59.3. Still Ryun stuck to his plan – surely the Kenyans would come back to him. Far from taking a breather, Keino overtook the tiring Jipcho and threw in a third lap of 58 seconds to lead Ryun, with a mere 300 metres to go, by an utterly unbridgeable six seconds – 40 metres and more. Ryun's despairing sprint was dramatic and courageous, and it took him from fifth to second place in less than half a lap. But he never got within fifteen metres of the leader, and when his sprint was spent he faded again, to finish a devastating twenty metres adrift.

Ryun did not give up. He carried on winning races outdoors and indoors, and even breaking records. By Munich in 1972 there were many who had him as favourite for the 1500 metres title. Once again, disaster struck. In his first-round heat he got into something of a tangle among two or three back-markers; there was no cause for alarm – one-and-a-half

laps still remained, and there were no real threats to his qualifying. But Ryun tried to squeeze himself into clear space between a tiring Ghanaian and a fading Pakistani, was simultaneously hit, spiked in the foot and tripped, and crashed to the track. It took him a good eight seconds to gather his wits, scramble to his feet and begin the chase, but by that time it was hopeless. The protest on his behalf failed, and he was out. The

Ryun in trouble: outpaced by Keino in Mexico (*above*); **stunned by a crashing fall in Munich, he vainly sets off in pursuit of the field.**

competition was poorer for his absence, and the eventual winner, Pekka Vasala, spoke for all the finalists in expressing regret that Ryun had not been there. 'Had he been, my tactics would have

been quite different,' said Vasala. It is a measure of great Olympians that even when they are not present their influence is somehow decisive.

But if Ryun has received sympathy and even a certain glory for his single Olympic silver medal in three Olympic campaigns, what of Ron Clarke? For half a dozen years in the 1960s Clarke was indisputably the best distance runner in the world. At one point he held the world record for three miles, 5000 metres, six miles, 10,000 metres, ten miles, 20,000 metres and one hour – something that even Paavo Nurmi had not managed at one and the same time.

He was, too, a magnificent racer, and his demolition of high class opposition in important races in his native Australia as well as in Europe and America was a familiar and crowd-pulling prospect throughout the Sixties. But in major championships, particularly in the Olympic Games, everything seemed to conspire against Clarke – poor reward for an athlete who, as a young nineteen-year-old miler, had carried the Olympic torch at the Melbourne opening ceremony.

It was Clarke's fate to be the finest possible upholder of the Zatopek-Kuts tradition of front-running at the precise moment at which coaches and athletes had discovered a combination of endurance and speed training that would render it vulnerable. It was his fate, too, to be at the height of his powers when the Games went to Mexico City, where even the best distance runners in the business would be at a cruel disadvantage. And finally it was his fate to be in the firing line when an unheralded tide of runners from Africa entered the Olympic arena to claim their share of the spoils.

In the 10,000 metres at Tokyo Clarke led the field into the final lap, a lap which was horribly congested by struggling lapped runners, only to be swallowed up in the final sprint by a hitherto unknown American-Indian, Billy Mills, and a hitherto unremarked Tunisian, Mohamed Gammoudi. In the 5000 metres he carried almost the whole field through most of the race, but he was never able to put them under enough pressure to string them out; with a lap and a half to go he lost all hope of retaining the initia-

Premature self-satisfaction: David Bedford (274) and Emiel Puttemans, well clear in the lead, discuss the possibility of attempting a world record in their 10,000 metres heat. In the Munich final both succumbed to the world-record pace of Lasse Viren.

tive as the fast finishers swept away from him, and he could finish in only ninth place, frustrated (oh, how he came to relive those frustrations) in the knowledge that he had won his heat in comfort rather quicker than Bob Schul won the final.

Three days later he led out the marathon field at a then unheard-of pace – well below five minutes per mile – and was still in the lead after fifteen kilometres in a still-unbelievable 45½ minutes. Once again the spirit had been brave but the flesh, or the preparation,

or perhaps just his luck, had not been up to it. He faded fast from contention in the face of Bikila's charge, and finished a disillusioned ninth in what remained the fastest marathon of his career. Three Olympic finals had given him one bronze medal.

In Mexico he knew things were going to be tough in the altitude and the heat. What he did not know was how much worse it was going to be for him and the other 'sea-level' men than it would be for the talented new Africans. As it was he plodded gamely along in the 10,000 metres with the leaders for twenty-one of the twenty-five laps; but those other leaders were all from Tunisia, Ethiopia or Kenya. Clarke's body literally ran out of oxygen, and as Naftali Temu and the rest ran away from him he struggled against his massive oxygen debt to reach the finish in a heroic sixth place and collapse in a heap, much to the consternation of his coach and the medical men hovering over him.

He was up out of his hospital bed the next morning, ready to join the heats and the final of the 5000 metres later in the week. Again, once the altitude, the Kenyans and Gammoudi had taken their toll in the first part of the race, the result was bound to be much the same, and Clarke finished fifth. Once again failure had been courageous and thoroughly honourable. Two more Olympic finals had produced no more medals.

Clarke's task at Tokyo had been difficult, as all Olympic tasks are difficult, particularly for favourites. He almost certainly underestimated the opposition in the 10,000 metres, he possibly lacked the commitment to test the rest of the field in the 5000 metres and he was probably ill-prepared for the marathon. His task at Mexico City was, in retrospect, well nigh impossible, and his performance in both races was beyond the call of duty. But even in three Empire and Commonwealth Games, despite a handful of silver medals, he was never strong enough or sharp enough or speedy enough on the day to win a title.

He left the stage without a gold medal, yet as a runner, an influence and a target he was to the sixties what Zatopek had been to the fifties. It was fitting, and just, and moving to a degree that on his way back from Mexico City to Australia Clarke stopped off in Prague to meet his old friend Emil Zatopek who, as they parted, handed the Australian a small parcel. Not wishing to open it on the spot and perhaps embarrass the giver, Clarke waited until he got home to look at his gift. It was Zatopek's Helsinki 10,000 metres gold medal.

Zatopek, the kindest of men, well knew the important difference between failure and not winning. In that sense Ron Clarke had not failed, and the Olympic Games were richer for him, as they had been for a man much closer to Zatopek even than Ron Clarke. Alain Mimoun was France's best distance runner in the very years that Zatopek was the world's best. When Zatopek won his first 10,000 metres gold medal, in London, Mimoun won his first silver. When

Champion at last: Alain Mimoun of France, three Olympic silver medals to his name in the shadow of Emil Zatopek, finally strikes gold in the Melbourne marathon with his old rival well back in the field.

Zatopek won the distance double at Brussels in the European Championships, Mimoun won both silvers. When Zatopek trounced Mimoun by $15\frac{1}{2}$ seconds in the Helsinki 10,000 metres, Mimoun beat the rest of the field by a further $15\frac{1}{2}$ seconds. And when Zatopek produced his inspired final lap to win the extraordinary 5000 metres later the same week, it was Mimoun who chased him to the line for yet another silver medal. If the late forties and early fifties had not been the years of Zatopek, they would almost certainly have been the years of Mimoun. By 1954, when Zatopek at last seemed to be on the wane, Mimoun was out of contention with a foot injury sustained when running on rough ground (he was, and remained well into middle age, a superb cross-country runner) and it looked as if he would end his career there and then, consigned to the records as the perpetual, gallant also-ran.

But in 1956, despite a gloomy prognosis for his foot, he was back at the Games, only to slump to his only bad result in an Olympic track race – twelfth place behind Kuts in a field of twenty-five in the 10,000 metres. And so to what could only be his last ever Olympic event, and his first attempt at the marathon, alongside his old rival Emil Zatopek.

Finally, at this last opportunity, the dog had his day, the Olympian received his reward. Mimoun was never out of the leading group while Zatopek, no longer at peak fitness, let them go away into the distance, abandoned his agonised rolling gait and even began to look as if he was enjoying his run. Mimoun was well in the lead eight miles from the finish, and he crossed the line a minute-and-a-half ahead of his nearest pursuers.

He did not take the blankets offered him, or do his lap of honour, or go off in search of his tracksuit. He waited by the finish to greet home the runner in sixth place, the runner he had never beaten before in his life. He met Zatopek on the line; they smiled and embraced each other.

Not every 'nearly man' has the opportunity, or the determination, or even the good fortune, to graduate to the ranks of the champions. When one does, the experience is doubly sweet.

The eternal flame

THERE WILL NEVER BE AN OLYMPIC GAMES WITHOUT SURPRISES.
Records will eventually be broken, as records always are. Heroics
will abound as long as the lure of an Olympic medal retains its
potency, and, for the same reason, so will deep and inconsolable
disappointment.

The Games will remain, regrettably, a worry to their organisers, a focus for political gesture, a lure for profiteers and a target for sniping critics of all shades of opinion. Each is something we have come to expect, and something the Games has, to a large extent, been able to surmount.

The new heroes, too, will inevitably be compared with those of the past, because they will always need the same resilience and self-confidence as their predecessors. There will still be men of determination and courage like David Hemery in 1968, who went into the 400 metres hurdles final, a final that had fallen to an American for the previous six consecutive Games, knowing that to win it he had to break the world record. He knew, too, that he had to run the first half of the race faster than anyone had ever run it before, and that if his legs or lungs couldn't cope with the challenge he was in for disaster. He broke his world record, and won his gold medal in unforgettable style.

There will be equally determined and courageous women, like Ann Packer in Tokyo, who turned in a European record in the 400 metres final and yet could only finish second. So she turned to her second-string event, the 800 metres, which she had run only five times before the Games; she paced herself better than the entire field, rounded them all in the last half-lap and broke the world record to win her gold medal.

There will be innovators like Dick Fosbury, the high jumper who felt so dissatisfied with the conventional style of jumping that he invented his own way of clearing the bar – propelling himself head-first and on to his back. He seemed to have a fair chance of breaking his neck at every attempt; but the style not only worked for him – winning him a gold medal at Mexico City – but established

itself as the preferred method for dozens of champions who followed him.

There will be athletes with the sheer guts to thrust themselves deliberately into certain pain without even the assurance that their gesture is going to work. It failed for Gordon Pirie in Melbourne as he ran himself to exhaustion in an attempt to wear down the invincible Vladimir Kuts; it succeeded for Murray Halberg in Rome as he risked everything by sprinting for home with almost a quarter of the 5000 metres final still to go.

There will be runners who spring from nowhere on to the Olympic stage and so capture the imagination of their fellow-countrymen that they become fathers to a new obsession – like Hannes Kolehmainen, whose victories in 1912 founded the long tradition of runners in Finland; or Abebe Bikila, winner of consecutive marathons in Rome and Tokyo, who heralded a new breed of distance runners in the African hills.

And there will be just a few super-athletes whom even those of us fortunate enough to have won Olympic medals still look back at with awe – those who have collected Olympic titles almost as a matter of course, who have stamped their own greatness on a Games or a series of Games, and whose names are inextricably linked with Olympic history – names like Blankers-Koen and Oerter, Nurmi and Viren, Owens and Zatopek.

After Los Angeles and Seoul, after the Games of 1992 and the centenary Olympics which must surely be staged in Athens in 1996, the list will be longer. The tales of heroism and triumph, despair and disaster will have been capped by new generations of Olympians, and the young athletes who have taken our place will still thrill, as we did, to the very thought of joining their ranks.

Index

Athletes who have represented their country are identified by the country's official Olympic initials. Coaches and others whose duties and influence have often extended beyond national boundaries are listed without national labels. Page numbers in italics refer to photographs.

Abrahams, Harold (GBR) *25*, *26*, *27*, 28, 31, 32, 57, 111
Akii-Bua, John (UGA) 125, 129, *130*, *131*
Amateur Athletic Association (AAA) 31
Amsterdam Olympic Games (1928) 31, 44, 57, 69, 122, 141
Andersson, Arne (SWE) 85
Antwerp Olympic Games (1920) 28, 41, 57, 78
Askola, Arvo (FIN) 44, *44*
Athens Olympic Games (1896) 25-6 33, 95
Avilov, Nikolai (URS) 143

Babka, Richard 'Rink' (USA) 114
Balas, Iolanda (ROM) 118
Bannister, Roger (GBR) *32-3*, 33, 95, 98
Bausch, James (USA) 139, 141
Bayi, Filbert (TAN) 106, 127, 129, *131*, 133
Beamon, Bob (USA) 65, *116*, 117-8
Beccali, Luigi (ITA) *30-1*, 32
Bedford, David (GBR) 36, 46, *47*, 91, *162*
Berlin Olympic Games (1936) 31-3, 36, 44, 57-9, 70, 141
Berutti, Livio (ITA) 60
Bignal *see* Rand
Bikila, Abebe (ETH) *120-1*, 122, *122-3*, 125, 133, 162, 165
Biwott, Amos (KEN) *124*, 127
Blake, Arthur (USA) 25
Blankers, Jan 71
Blankers-Koen, Fanny (HOL) *66-7*, *68*, 70, 70-3, *71*, *72-3*, 77, 78, 114, 165
Boit, Mike (KEN) 127, 133
Bolotnikov, Pyotr (URS) 83, 90-1, *91*, 98, 100
Bonthron, Bill (USA) 32
Borzov, Valery (URS) 65
Boston, Ralph (USA) 117

Bouin, Jean (FRA) 37, 41, *154*, *155*, 156
Boyle, Raelene (AUS) 79, 95, 156
Brasher, Christopher (GBR) *32-3*, 33, 95, 98
British Amateur Athletics Federation, 15
British Olympic Committee 15
Burghley, David, Lord (later Marquess of Exeter) (GBR) *28*, 31
Busse, Andreas (GDR) *18*, *19*

Calhoun, Lee (USA) 60
Cambridge University A.C. 26, 31
Carlisle School for Indians, Pennsylvania 139
Carlos, John (USA) 65
Carr, Henry (USA) 62
Carr, William (USA) 31
Carter, President Jimmy 12, 65, 106
Cartmell, Nathaniel (USA) 156
Cerutty, Percy *94*, 95-7, 98, 102
Chariots of Fire 28
Chataway, Christopher (GBR) *32-3*, 33, 86, *87*, *87*, 89, 95, 157
Chudina, Alexandra (URS) 74, 95
Clarke, Ronald (AUS) 91, 104, 124, *152-3*, 157, *158*, *159*, 162-3
Coe, Peter 10
Coe, Sebastian (GBR) *8-9*, 10-21, 15, *16*, *17*, *18*, *19*, *20*, *21*, 158
Coghlan, Eamonn (IRL) *104*
Cornes, J.F. 'Jerry' (GBR) *29*, 31-2
de Coubertin, Baron Pierre 28, 69, 137, 154
Crump, Jack 72
Cunningham, Glenn (USA) *30-1*, 32-3
Cuthbert, Betty (AUS) 95

Danek, Ludvik (TCH) 114, 117
Davies, Lynn (GBR) 117
Davis, Otis (USA) 62
Delany, Ron (IRL) 98
Desyachikov, Aleksei (URS) *91*
Didrikson, Mildred 'Babe' (USA) 69-70, *69*, 78, 118
Dillard, Harrison (USA) 60, *60-1*, 65
Dixon, Rodney (NZL) 48, 51, 104, 106, *106*, 154, 158
Doubell, Ralph (AUS) *102-3*, 104

Eastman, Ben (USA) 30-1
Elevaara, Jouko 50-1
Elliott, Herbert (AUS) *92-3*, *94*, 95, 96, 97, 98, 102, 158

El Ouafi, Boughèra (FRA) 122
Evans, Lee (USA) 11, 62, 65
Ewell, H. Norwood 'Barney' (USA) 60, *60-1*

Farrell, Tom (USA) *102-3*
Ferrell, Barbara (USA) 77
Finnish Olympic Committee 43
Flack, Edwin 'Ted' (AUS) 25-6, 95
Fosbury, Dick (USA) 165
Foster, Brendan (GBR) 15, 46, 48, 91, 129
Foster, Jack (NZL) 104-6

Gammoudi, Mohamed (TUN) 46, 124, *125*, *127*, 157, 162, 163
Gardner, Maureen (GBR) 70-1, *72*
Gentile, Giuseppe (ITA) 118
Goebbels, Josef 58
Gordien, Fortune (USA) 114
Gordon, Edward (USA) 57
Grace, Dr William Gilbert 139
Greene, Charlie (USA) *63*
Grodotzki, Hans (GER) 100, 156
Guillemot, Joseph (FRA) *40*, 41

Haase, Jurgen (GDR) 36
Haggman, Pirjo (FIN) 50
Hahn, Archie (USA) 156
Halberg, Murray (NZL) 97, 98, 102, 156, 165
Haro, Mariano (ESP) 47
Hary, Armin (GER) 60
Hayes, Bob (USA) 62, *62*, 65
Heino, Viljo (FIN) 85
Helsinki Olympic Games (1952) 36, 38, 44-5, 60, 74, 78, 86, 113
Hemery, David (GBR) 10, *10*, 165
Hildenbrand, Klaus-Peter (GER) *51*
Hines, Jim (USA) *63*
Hingsen, Jurgen (GER) 146
Hitler, Adolf 58
Hitomi, Kinue (JPN) 69
Hockert, Gunnar (FIN) 44
Hubbard, William de Hart (USA) 54
de la Hunty (Strickland), Shirley (AUS) 95

Ibbotson, Derek (GBR) 90, *90*
Igloi, Mihaly 45, 156
Iharos, Sandor (HUN) 157
International Olympic Committee (IOC) 15, 78, 124, 131, 139
Iso-Hollo, Volmari (FIN) 44, *44*

Jackson, Marjorie (AUS) 95
Jansson, Gustav (SWE) 88
Jarvinen, Akilles (FIN) 141
Jazy, Michel (FRA) *95*, 98
Jenkins, Charley (USA) 62
Jenner, Bruce (USA) *140-1, 142*, 143
Jipcho, Ben (KEN) 125, 127, 129, *129*, 131, 133, 160
Johnson, Rafer (USA) 143
Jones, Hayes (USA) 62
Juantorena, Alberto (CUB) 11-12, *11*, 156

Kachanov, Valery (URS) 146
Keino, Kipchoge (KEN) *48, 49, 106*, 124, 125, *126-7, 127, 128-9*, 133, 154, 158, 160, *160*
Kerr, George (JAM*) *98-9*, 100, 102
Kipkurgat, John (KEN) 127
Kiprugut, Wilson (KEN) *102-3*, 122
Kirszenstein *see* Szewinska
Kolehmainen, Hannes (FIN) *37*, 38-41, 44, 45, 51, 78, *154*, 156, 165
Kolehmainen, Tatu (FIN) 38, 41
Kolehmainen, Viljami 'Willie' (FIN) 38
Kozakiewicz, Wladýslaw (POL) 19
Kratschmer, Guido (GER) 146
Kuts, Vladimir (URS) 33, 83, 85, 88-91, *89, 90, 91*, 133, 157, 162, 163, 165

La Beach, Lloyd (PAN) *60-1*
Lamy, Jennifer (AUS) 79
Landy, John (AUS) 95, 97, 98
Laufer, Heinz (GER) 33
Lehtinen, Lauri (FIN) 44, *44*
Lermusiaux, Albin (FRA) 25
Liddell, Eric (GBR) *24, 26, 28*, 31
Liimatainen, Heikki (FIN) 44
Lillak, Tiina (FIN) 50
Lincoln, Mervyn (AUS) 98
London Olympic Games (1908) 38
London Olympic Games (1948) 44, 60, 70-2, 85, 141-3, 146
Los Angeles Olympic Games (1932) 30, 31-2, 44, 54, 57, 69-70, 139, 141
Los Angeles Olympic Games (1984) 65, 69, 78, 165
Louis, Spiridon (GRE) 33
Loukola, Toivo (FIN) 44
Lovelock, Jack (NZL) *22-3, 29, 30-1*, 31-3, 95, 100, 106

*George Kerr competed in the colours of the combined British West Indies team in 1960 and for Jamaica in 1964

Lydiard, Arthur, 45, 46, 97, 98, 100, 102, 104, 106

Maaninka, Kaarlo (FIN) 50-1, 133
MacArthur, General Douglas 57
McCorquodale, Alistair (GBR) *60-1*
Macdonald, Linsey (GBR) 15
McDonald Bailey, Emmanuel (GBR) *60-1*
McKenley, Herbert (JAM) 60
Malinowski, Bronislaw (POL) 133
Mathias, Bob (USA) *138, 139*, 143
Melbourne Hare and Hounds A.C. 25
Melbourne Olympic Games (1956) 33, 44, 45, 60, 62, 89-90, 95, 114, 143, 156-8, 162, 163, *164-5*
Mennea, Pietro (ITA) *12-3*, 19
Metcalfe, Ralph (USA) 57, *57*, 58
Mexico City Olympic Games (1968) 10, 44, 45, 62-5, 76, 77, 104, 114, 117, 124-5, 133, 143, 160, 162-3, 165
Meyfarth, Ulrike (GER) 118
Miller, Lennox (JAM) *63*
Mills, Billy (USA) 124, *157*, 162
Mimoun, Alain (Ali Mimoun O Kacha) (FRA) *86-7, 86, 87*, 122, 157, 163, *163*
Moens, Roger (BEL) 98, 100, 102, 154, *156*
Montreal Olympic Games (1976) 11-2, 46-8, 50, 77, 106, 118, 127-31, 143, 156
Morris, Glenn (USA) 141
Morrow, Bobby Joe (USA) 60
Moscow Olympic Games (1980) 10-21, 50, 106, 118, 131, 133, 150, 158
Moses, Edwin (USA) 65, 129, 143
Munich Olympic Games (1972) 10-11, 45, 46, 76-7, 104, 118, 125, 154, 156, 158, 160
Mussabini, Sam 28, 111

Nicholas, HRH Prince of Greece 25
Niskanen, Onni 122
Noel-Baker, Philip (GBR) 26
Norman, Peter (AUS) 65
Nurmi, Paavo (FIN) *35, 38, 39, 40*, 41-5, *41, 42-3*, 51, 72, 78, 162, 165

Odam *see* Tyler
Oerter, Al (USA) *108-9, 111, 112, 113*, 114-7, *114, 115*, 118, 165
Osborn, Harold (USA) 139
Ovett, Steve (GBR) 12, 15, *16, 17, 18, 19*, 137, 158

Owens, James Cleveland 'Jesse' (USA) *52-3, 55, 56, 57, 57-8, 58-9*, 65, 72, *72*, 113, 165
Oxford University A.C. 26, 31

Packer, Ann (GBR) *75*, 165
Paddock, Charles (USA) 26
Paris Olympic Games (1924) 26, 27, 28, 31, 43, 54, 57, 111
Patton, Melvin (USA) 60, *60-1*
Pennsylvania University 31
Peters, Jim (GBR) 88
Peters, Mary (GBR) 76-7, *77*
Pietri, Dorando (ITA) 38
Pirie, Gordon (GBR) 86, *86*, 89-90, *90*, 165
Porritt, Arthur (NZL) 27
Prefontaine, Steve (USA) 46, *46*
Press, Irina (URS) 74, *74*
Princeton University 32
Prudencio, Nelson (BRA) 118
Puttemans, Emiel (BEL) 11, 46, 47, 91, *162*

Quax, Dick (NZL) 48, *51*, 106, *107*

Radke, Lina (GER) 69
Rand (Bignal), Mary (GBR) 74, 75, *75*, 76
Reiff, Gaston (BEL) *82-3, 83, 84, 85*, 86
Remigino, Lindy (USA) 60
Rhadi ben Abdesselem (MAR) 122, *123*
Richards, Bob (USA) 118
Riefenstahl, Leni 58
Ritola, Ville (FIN) *41*, 43-4
Robertson, George (GBR) 25
Robinson, Matthew 'Mack' (USA) 58
Rome Olympic Games (1960) 60, 62, 74, 90-1, 98-102, 114, 117, 122, 143, 154, 156, 165
Rono, Henry (KEN) 131, 133
Rosendahl, Heide (GER) 76-7, *76*
Rozsavolgyi, Istvan (HUN) 95, 157
Rudolph, Wilma (USA) *65*
Ryun, Jim (USA) 125, 158-62, *160-1*

St Louis Olympic Games (1904) 137, 156
Salminen, Ilmari (FIN) 44, *44*
Saneyev, Viktor (URS) *117*, 118, *118*, *119*
Schade, Herbert (GER) 86, 87, *87*
Schmidt, Jozef (POL) 118
Scholz, Jackson (USA) *26, 27*
Schul, Bob (USA) 162

Sherwood, John (GBR) 10
Sherwood, Sheila (GBR) 10
Shiley, Jean (USA) 70
Shorter, Frank (USA) 46
Simpson, George (USA) 57
Slijkhuis, Willem (HOL) 83, 85
Smith, Tommie (USA) *64*, 65
Snell, Peter (NZL) 97, *98-9*, 100-2,
    100, *101*, 106, 122, 154, *156*
Stampfl, Franz 95, 98, 102
Stanfield, Andy (USA) 60
Stanford University 30
Stecher, Renate (GDR) 156
Stewart, Ian (GBR) 46
Stockholm Olympic Games (1912) 26,
    38-41, 137-9, 146, 156, 165
Straub, Jurgen (GDR) 19, 20, *20*
Strickland *see* de la Hunty
Strode-Jackson, Arnold (GBR) 26
Sylvester, Jay (USA) *115*, 117
Szewinska (Kirszenstein), Irina (POL)
    77-8, *78*, *79*

Tabori, Laszlo (HUN) 157
Temu, Naftali (KEN) 125, *127*, 162
Ter-Ovanesyan, Igor (URS) 117
Thompson, Daley (GBR) 15, *134-5*,
    137, 143-6, *143*, *144-9*, 150, *150-1*
Thompson, Ian (GBR) 106
Thorpe, Jim (USA) *136*, *137*, 139, 146
Tokyo Olympic Games (1964) 60, 62,
    74, 75, 76, 102, 114-7, 122, 158, 162,
    165

Tolan, Thomas 'Eddie' (USA) 54, *54*,
57
Toomey, Bill (USA) 143
Tulloh, Bruce (GBR) 102
Tyler (Odam), Dorothy (GBR) 118,
156
Tyus, Wyomia (USA) 77

United States Women's Amateur
    Athletic Union 69
University of California, Los Angeles
    (UCLA) 143
Uudmäe, Jaak (URS) 118

Vaatainen, Juha (FIN) 36, *36*, 45, *45*
Van Damme, Ivo (BEL) *104-5*, 156
Vasala, Pekka (FIN) 45, *48*, *49*, 127,
    154, 160
Victoria Amateur Athletic Association
    95
Viren, Lasse (FIN) 11, 19, *34*, 45, 46,
    46-8, *47*, 48, *50*, 51, *51*, 78, 106, *107*,
    125, 129, *132-3*, 133, 143, 162, 165

Walker, Arthur (USA) 118
Walker, John (NZL) 12, *104-5*, 106,
    129, 156
Wellmann, Paul-Heinz (GER) *104-5*
Wells, Allan (GBR) 12, *13*, *14*, 17, 19
Williams, Yvette (NZL) 95, *110*, 113-4
Wilson, Harry 12
Wolde, Mamo (ETH) 124, 125, *125*
Wooderson, Sydney (GBR) 32, 83

Yang, C.K. (Yang Chuan-kwang)
    (ROC) 143
Yifter, Miruts (ETH) 19, 50, 78, 125,
    129, 131, *132-3*, 133
Yrjola, Paavo (FIN) 141

Zatopek, Emil (TCH) 48, 78, *80-1*, *82*,
    83-9, *83-7*, 91, 133, 157, 162, 163,
    165
Zhukov, Evgeny (URS) *91*.

KEY

AUS – Australia; BEL – Belgium; BRA
– Brazil; CAN – Canada; CUB – Cuba;
ESP – Spain; ETH – Ethiopa; FIN –
Finland; FRA – France; GBR – Great
Britain and Northern Ireland; GDR –
German Democratic Republic (from
1968); GER – Germany (up to 1964),
German Federal Republic (since 1968);
GRE – Greece; HOL – Netherlands;
HUN – Hungary; IRL – Ireland; ITA
– Italy; JAM – Jamaica; JPN – Japan;
KEN – Kenya; MAR – Morocco; NZL
– New Zealand; PAN – Panama; POL –
Poland; ROC – Republic of China (Tai-
wan); ROM – Romania; SWE – Sweden;
TAN – Tanzania; TCH – Czechoslo-
vakia; TUN – Tunisia; UGA – Uganda;
URS – U.S.S.R.; USA – United States
of America.